Been There, Undone That

Howard W. Streiffer

Published by Howard W. Streiffer, 2026.

BEEN THERE, UNDONE THAT

First edition. April 30, 2026.

ISBN: 979-8227624062

Written by Howard W. Streiffer.

Table of Contents

DISCLAIMER

I FEEL I HAVE GAINED a great deal of insight into principles and strategies for dealing with anxiety over my 70 years of struggling with it, and I would like to share these with others who struggle with emotional or psychological issues to help them make their lives better. Please be aware that I am not a medical or mental health professional and that I would certainly encourage you to seek guidance from such folks before taking any potentially life-changing actions. Also, my suggestions do not relate to more complex mental issues such as schizophrenia, bipolar disorders, PTSD, etc., with which I have had no experience.

DEDICATION

I FEEL EXTREMELY FORTUNATE to be able to dedicate this book to my family:

To my wife, Cheryl, I offer very special thanks. The work on this book would <u>never</u> have been possible without the amazing support and help you so willingly provide every day, not just to me but to our children, other family members, and friends. I constantly marvel at how much you do for so many. There is a little-known story about how Mrs. Norman Vincent Peale did so many things for her husband, thereby allowing the well-known motivational and positive thinking author and minister to concentrate on his passion and calling. I often think that you make her look like a narcissist! I could not do most of the things I am able to do without all of the many things you do for us all. I eternally appreciate your support and help. You are an incredible friend and wife, loving and talented beyond measure.

To our four children: You have been, and are, the light of my life! Each of you is unique and wonderful. I will always remember and cherish our great times together and watching you grow into the incredible people you are today. I am proud of each of you ... beyond words!

To paraphrase an old friend of mine, my children were very lucky – they inherited their good looks from their mothers and their intelligence from my wives.

To Michelle, you always have my support and appreciation. This book would not have been possible without you as well.

Finally, to my parents: They, to the absolute best of their ability, provided all the love, support, and opportunities that my brother and I enjoyed. To them I am eternally grateful.

ACKNOWLEDGEMENTS

MARLY, YOUR UNDERSTANDING, input, patience, and professional support throughout the bulk of the time I was writing this book have been of inestimable value not only to this book, but to so many other phases of my life as well.

And to Brian Mizuki, Psy.D., go my eternal thanks for his extremely valuable key suggestion to remove my head from the sand and the minutia and to get some of the help noted below. Without this intelligent redirection, I may never have been able to get to the finish line, but instead would still be lost in the weeds.

The quality and quantity of the suggested changes made by Elizabeth Zack, Chris Streiffer, Danika Marzluff, Arlene Bazin, John and Barbara Little, and Mary Bailey made significant improvements in this work. While I was unable to implement all the suggestions any one of you made, many are reflected in the book and provided substantive upgrades.

Brenda Lewis, you have been such an <u>amazing</u> assistant! You have given me the time to work on other parts of the book and thereby have helped make everything I have written much better. You are living proof that, in fact, you **can** make chicken salad out of chicken scratch!

Cover photo taken by Katie Streiffer, August 2021, in the Grand Teton National Park.

PREFACE

SOMETIME CLOSE TO MY seventieth birthday, it dawned on me that I had spent most of the last sixty years doing everything I possibly could to hide from almost everyone I knew a very significant part of myself, my life, and my challenges. By nature, I am a rather private person, and when I was growing up, I was ashamed of having an anxiety problem that I considered a personal weakness. So I began living a life which I built around hiding this issue from everyone but my immediate family.

Concealing my mental struggles with anxiety and depression has involved a great deal of effort; it was quite a burden! In writing and publishing this book, I am blowing away a carefully crafted and diligently fostered personal image that I cultivated now for almost seven decades. This is somewhat fraught with danger for me from a mental health standpoint: Most folks don't easily throw away this much effort or casually risk dealing with a huge helping of rejection and potential embarrassment, especially if it turns out there is no interest in the book, or if it helps no one.

But I am excited to take the risk because the potential for good is so high. If this publication can help others have better, more productive, and happier lives, which I hope and believe is very possible, I will have fulfilled what I feel is my reason for being and for enduring the hardships I have faced.

I also would like to acknowledge that, while deciding to open up about my issues required a significant adjustment in my thinking, the actual process of writing transparently about my life, the insights I've had, and the changes I've made, has resulted in my experiencing a very significant feeling of relief, catharsis, and peace. So, I believe I ended up doing the right thing! During my seventy-plus years of intense self-help and professional work in dealing with issues like anxiety, fear, depression, stress, sleep deprivation, and more, I learned a considerable amount about how to have a happier and less stressful, yet more successful and productive life. Better personal relationships also resulted from these accomplishments. It took considerable work to make the improvements, but I am certain that my current life is incredibly richer, more peaceful, and more productive than it was previously or would have been without this lifetime of concentrated work, learning, and changing.

My approach to writing this book is definitely not a dogmatic "my way or the highway" approach. I simply want to present concepts and techniques I have tried and found helpful. They have all worked for me, and I am presenting the information which I believe would be of help to others. I sincerely believe there is information here that would be useful to virtually all readers. This book is my attempt to pass along as much information as possible so others can learn, grow, and evolve more quickly than I did, and experience much less anxiety.

I hope you will try some of these ideas, taking the ones that resonate best with you and making them your own...then go on to try others.

When I first thought of listing the tools I had available to me to combat anxiety, I came up with 19, and I felt rich with options! Realizing that I had such a number of different strategies and ideas helped me a lot. Now, after expanding the list fully and including principles and strategies, I am very pleased to realize that there are two to three times this initial amount with well over 100 additional thoughts or suggestions for your consideration.

Some people believe that "fifty cannot talk to twenty;" but I totally disagree: OF COURSE we can learn from those who have had somewhat different experiences and are of different ages! Someone who is twenty years of age can learn much from someone who is older, if they are motivated or willing to listen... even if they don't yet have the same variety of experiences in their lives.

At one or more times in all of our lives, every single one of us has benefitted from the knowledge and experience of people who have come before us. If you beg to differ, let me ask a simple question: Did your parents teach you anything when you were a child that you have retained, and which has made your life better? My hope now is that you, in your adult life, will benefit from the lessons I have learned after much reading, work, and help.

You see, as I have aged (and aged!), the most satisfying aspect in my life has become being able to help others lead more productive lives with much less pain, stress, and anxiety. This has become my goal for my remaining years on this earth. This desire to help others learn in a much timelier fashion than what took me seventy years to master is my purpose today and for the future.

I fully intend to be as successful with this as with the other goals I held in my earlier years.

My sincere desire is to provide anyone suffering from excessive anxiety and stress with information and tools to combat these conditions. I genuinely want to give to you what was not available to me when I was in my 20's. I would have given anything for this book at that time!

So, I implore you to let me help jump-start you along your own journey to experiencing more happiness, fulfillment, gratitude, contentment, and productivity in your life. Please accept my gift to you which has taken me a lifetime to acquire, so you will benefit sooner and enjoy the benefits longer.

-Howard Streiffer, age 82, March 2026

GUARANTEE

I HAVE SPENT LITERALLY thousands of hours working on and with the material contained in this book. I assure you that I would not have done this or taken the substantial additional time to write this book if I did not believe 150% in what I say. That being the case, I give you this guarantee:

If you read this book fully and give a fair trial of the principles and strategies described, yet feel you have not gotten your money's worth, I will see that you are reimbursed the full price that you paid after you demonstrate compliance with the simple conditions above.

INTRODUCTION

STRESS! It is prevalent in so many aspects of society today, with anxiety and depression as some of its offspring. Anxiety disorders are on a rapid and extremely dangerous rise in our society. According to the Anxiety and Depression Association of America, approximately 19% of U.S. adults suffer from anxiety disorders. (As of this writing, this equates to 57 million citizens!) One of the sad and extremely disturbing aspects of this mental health issue is that it is seriously affecting children as well.

Each and every day we learn more about the harmful effects of stress and mental illness. Put simply, stress can detract from our enjoyment, rob us of happiness, and even shorten our lives! It is unquestionably a topic worthy of consideration.

As I know something on a personal level about the suffering related to anxiety, I have made it my goal to contribute to lessening this horrible burden that affects the rich, poor, famous, infamous, artists, athletes, elderly, children, and all those other regular folks like you and me. Combatting the negative effects of stress will be the main focus of *Been There, Undone That* (because I have BEEN there and yet I went on to UNDO that, happily), and you can apply the forthcoming techniques and principles to experiences with negative thinking, fear, guilt, shame, and/or depression, if you so choose.

Before I begin, I want to acknowledge that there are both good and bad types of stress. Good stress may push us to succeed or help us achieve positive goals. And while there may be a relatively small group of people who end up overly stimulated by good things, it does not compare to the often severe consequences of negative or bad stress, which can rob us of joy and happiness by causing panic attacks, depression, etc.

The many emotional challenges and negative thoughts I had because of my issues led me to formulate many principles and strategies to deal and cope with them more effectively and with better results.

My battles with severe anxiety and related matters began in my early childhood; and while on the one hand that is an unfortunate fact, I also am happy about my efforts to get beyond the problems, the progress I made, and the self-knowledge I gleaned along this journey. The work I've done has made tremendous positive differences in both my personal and professional lives, adding immeasurably to my quality of life.

> **If I had known at age twenty what I know at age eighty, my life would have been SO much happier and less filled with anxiety, stress, angst, and more! This is what I very much want to give to you.**

I very much want to help others get through these issues more quickly and easily than I have—and I am in a position today to do so. Please stick with me. Let me show you how to tweak and alter some parameters in your life so that you too can experience more of life's beauty and joy.

I have been where many others are now, and there are better ways to go through life than those we often put ourselves through. Friends, it is achievable! We can choose to change our debilitating thought patterns and choices so that we keep from falling into stress, pain, and anxiety-filled traps that keep us stuck.

WHY THIS BOOK IS UNIQUE

The concepts explained here work towards reducing those experiences of anxiety, stress, negativity, inertia, and self-defeatism. Sure, there are hundreds (thousands?) of books on healing written by professionals in the mental health field, the objective of which is to help those with such problems get better and overcome the negative impact and stress they can have on our lives. Yet this book is written from the point of view of the "lab rat," so to speak, or the affected person—the one who is suffering in the trenches every single day, and simply going through the maze of everyday life hoping to find something or someone to "help me make it through the night!"

You should know that while I refer to myself as a lab rat from time to time, I do like to picture myself as being at least a smart rat (maybe even one who's cute and fuzzy on my better days). For as it turned out, I am quite capable of learning, albeit slowly at times.

For those of you who might not relish the thought of any kind of rat, think of me instead as your personal research assistant. For well over half a century I've worked very hard to develop, try, adjust, and find principles and strategies that work to reduce anxiety, depression, and stress. In the pages of this book, I share my lifetime of work with those most in need of taming their demons and moving towards more happiness and contentment.

And to these doubters who feel that folks just do not change, I say this extremely negative view disavows the benefits of passing along learning in general, good parenting, role models, mentoring, the idea of therapy, and so on. I subscribe fully to the argument that people can and will change if they have the motivation to do so; and my core belief on the subject is that having older, more experienced, and wiser people pass along their insights is a key link in the educational chain.

Also, we have probably all heard of the concept that the normal person uses only a fraction of their brain (usually the 10% figure is bandied about). Regardless of how accurate that percentage is, I think it is a given that we don't make full use of our minds; and for practical purposes we could all make better use of this incredible tool. For instance, I believe that improper thinking and the way we allow ourselves to be burdened by stress, anxiety, and lack of productivity is a good example of not fully utilizing our minds in the best ways.

Moreover, I also subscribe to the general theory that stress and anxiety tend to decrease with age because we learn and have different experiences over time. Simply put, as we age, we learn to adapt. Whether it is due to our anxiety responses not being activated because we have learned to cope better, or whether it is because we really just don't give a damn, the general arc of our personal universe is moving toward calmness!

But why do it yourself and wait for aging to acquire insights on living completely? Who really wants to wait that long to really begin to live — wouldn't it be nicer to begin sooner?

THE TRUTHS IN THIS BOOK

As for the ideas contained within this book, I know they have been invaluable to me and they certainly have value for millions of others! They are also teachable.

This is not a theory book, and the ideas contained within are not ones I just made up on the fly. I have field-tested everything as the lab rat and included only those ideas and techniques I personally found helpful.

I also am not including them simply because I read them somewhere; once again, I have used them all, and still do (for the most part). I genuinely want to share them with anyone who is interested, knowing that they have been of great benefit to me.

Much of our stress and pain in life comes from inexperience; from not knowing what works in given situations. Yet this can be a lot like joining an exercise class: You do not know what to do or how to do it at first, and then after watching, listening, and practicing, you figure it all out. Life can be similar, so one purpose of this book is to give you the tools to deal with situations more quickly than you might figure out on your own. When people are weighed down with anxiety, fear, shame, guilt, thoughts centered around ego, or negative and debilitating thoughts, they tend to limit their horizons and have a less full and productive life than is possible.

———————◉———————

AT THE END OF THE DAY

Do you believe that being happier and more productive will increase a person's creativity and the overall range of their thought processes? I do! Most people want to achieve a more productive, more successful, and happier life with less stress and effort. Many people believe that this is not in the realm of possibility for them; but let me disagree. We can all achieve this goal or at least make considerable progress in this regard by following practices that you find work for you.

At the end of the day, what is important as you read this book is for you to:

> Set aside, at least temporarily, any ideas you encounter which do not resonate with you.

> Decide which ideas are appealing and might be helpful to you;

> Consider which ideas you might want to change to make them more your own;

> Choose some ideas to try out in your life;

> Give those ideas a fair trial; and

> Permanently adopt the ideas that are effective for you.

And here is another word of advice before we get to the heart of the matter. Please keep in mind that this book is not intended as a speed-reading exercise. If you read it thoughtfully, taking your time to consider the ideas, this book should help you breathe in and absorb the important points. Allow some time for the thoughts about being willing to do things differently to become part of you. If you tend to fight change, as many of us do, it may require you to work diligently at being more open-minded; for in this case, to fight change is to fight progress and self-improvement. Instead, go about improving your daily actions and thought processes.

Finally, while I have experienced some scary and debilitating times and had to go through numerous setbacks, I have always tried extremely hard to never let my disabilities hold me back or keep me from trying to do what I felt I should be capable of accomplishing, be these physical or mental challenges. This was exceedingly difficult to do at times, but I also had an extraordinarily powerful desire to accomplish my goals, get better, and find peace. It is my hope that this book will inspire others to do the same—to keep trying no matter their circumstances or setbacks.

My fellow travelers, motivate yourself to get started by asking yourself the following:

> Do I want to try to make my life better?

> Do I yearn for stronger and more meaningful relationships?

> Do I desire less internal stress, negative self-talk, regret, shame, anger, guilt, misery, lack of confidence, etc.?

> Do I wish to find more peace, love, success, and positive feelings, such as happiness, joy, and contentment?

If the answer for you is the same as it was for me—a resounding **"YES!"** to every one of these questions—then I hope you will agree that the continuing effort is well worth it.

So don't think of the essential principles and specific strategies contained within as work; **think of them as doing something for yourself that will provide benefits beyond measure.**

PART I

YOU'RE NOT BROKEN OR DAMAGED. YOU ARE A NORMAL, FLAWED MEMBER OF THE HUMAN RACE!

PART I - OVERVIEW

HAVE YOU EVER GIVEN any thought to the number of facets we all have within our incredible and intricate personalities? It is almost limitless, as we are complex beings with individual strengths, weaknesses, and flaws. There is no one who qualifies as "normal" across the entire spectrum of personality attributes.

You may be familiar with the term, "the new normal," but the reality is, if you consider all of man's traits, it is more like there is NO normal! This is by no means a bad thing: What would life be like if we were all dead centered on the bell curves for every personality trait? Not only would life be extremely boring, but there would also be no progress. (Also, there would be no bell curve!) It is the outliers who really move us along, many of whom have been highly driven or even compulsive.

Just as it is with wood and leather, it is the infinite nuances of grain, irregularities, and imperfections that contribute to the beautiful and wonderful complexities of our character and uniqueness, and make us who we are. However, we may also agree that some of these nuances are not so wonderful. Some create serious issues, suffering, stress, and unhappiness.

Wouldn't it be wonderful if we could find ways to reduce our own suffering, and that of our fellow humans? While this is a rather lofty and difficult goal to achieve, contributing to that end is, nevertheless, one of the main goals of this book.

CHAPTER 1

OUR INCREDIBLE AND INTRICATE PERSONALITIES

RADICAL IDEA

Here is a very radical thought for you: You may well be as normal as anyone you know! In all likelihood, you may have some things to tweak and work on, but overall, you are probably a fine person trying to just make it through the day and improve who you are and how you deal with life. Stop assuming you are alone and totally broken, damaged, abnormal, and screwed up while everyone else is simply fine. T'ain't so ... on either side of that comparison.

Certainly not everyone else is fine! It's time to recognize, if you haven't already, that EVERYONE has weaknesses, and no one is normal in all aspects. Someone has pointed out that to be human is to be broken. That is just the way it is—no one is perfect. Put slightly differently, who do you know who doesn't have a few issues to work on?

So that means almost certainly you are not the terrible or catastrophically flawed Attila the Hun you may think you are. You are just a normal, flawed human being; and perhaps you don't let others get to know the real you because you're ashamed of who you are and have a poor self-image. But the odds are strong that, despite what you might think about yourself, you are a cool, multi–faceted person with numerous great qualities. And if you screw up from time to time, welcome to the human race!

As a member of humanity, you may tend to react in certain ways to specific stimuli, including the things others say or do. That's something we all do; and in all likelihood, some of these reactions may not be productive. For instance, they may cause delays, hurt, or pain, and/or confusion. And if I were to grill you on your common reactions or patterns of responding to

16

certain people, stimuli, or situations, you might end up saying, "That's just how my mind works!"

Okay, so it is—or perhaps more appropriately, that's just how it has been up to this point. But you can CHANGE all that!

REINING IN YOUR MENTAL REFLEXES

Please DON'T tell me you can't change; I know from personal experience, and from talking with others, that excuses like "the devil made me do it," "that's just the way I am," and "it's a knee-jerk reaction" are simply NOT valid. If they were, I would not be wasting my time writing this book! And my book is not called *Been There, Undone That* for no reason. You can *un*do it, or in this case, redo it ...You CAN change!

The whole point, and possibly the most important point in this book, is that unlike certain physical reflexes which we cannot control, we actually can control our mental reflexes. In a sense, this is just another way of saying that we can control how and what we think and the choices we make in our lives.

Some of these changes may require a little time and practice, but so what? I mean, really, if you have thought patterns in your life that cause you problems, misery, reduced productivity, or diminished quality in your relationships, what could be better or more important than to change these? It is sort of like the feeling you get when you stop hitting yourself on the head with a hammer. That new lack of pain is nice, and you can also revel now in the addition of joy and laughter to your life, as well as the positive affirmations and endorphins generated by seeing the changes that are taking place.

> **We can all change if we are truly motivated to do so!**

You may have conflicting goals, attitudes, hopes, needs, and so on—we all do—but if you really want to change, you can. And please do not swear that you have "passionately wanted to change" a certain trait over time, but despite this feeling, you have remained unchanged. All that is just a sign of conflicting goals. It certainly does not mean you can't change!

LET ME WEIGH IN

Let me give you a good example of why you should believe me here: In the past I thought about and typed up 14 pages of all the reasons I really wanted and needed to lose weight, the ways I could achieve this transformation, as well as the benefits I knew I could achieve by succeeding; but guess what? I didn't! I had myself thoroughly convinced that I REALLY wanted to lose weight—until one day it finally dawned on me that despite my heartfelt protestations, I had conflicting needs or desires which I had to resolve before I could lose weight.

I'm going to further illustrate this revelation with a relatively stark realization: If someone had literally followed me around 24/7 with a gun to my head telling me I was to lose weight, and if I absolutely knew that he would pull the trigger if I touched any sweets, do you think I would be able to give them up completely? I assure you that **I COULD, and I WOULD** in a New York second! My not losing weight was just a matter of my true motivation not being as strong as it could be, because of other conflicting desires that were in play.

Let me start though by mentioning that I do not drink wine, beer, or liquor. I do not use any non-prescription drugs, smoke, hunt, fish, sail, surf, fly, or golf. Also, my racquetball, tennis, and pickleball days are over, due to a deteriorating shoulder. And while I have some appreciation for music and art, they are not passionate feelings; and in general, I am not an artsy or a museum person. So, food, eating, and enjoyment, both with family and friends, is a significant source of happiness, comfort, and pleasure for me. In fact, I have many warm, loving, social memories of good times involving food! Plus, I was born with a world-class, voracious, industrial strength sweet tooth!

So yes, I had quite a hurdle to clear before my rational mind could utilize my 14 pages of notes on why I should go about losing weight.

FRESH EYES

Now I'd like to ask you to apply this same kind of thinking to yourself and to one of your own as-yet-to-be-accomplished goals. As you look at your previous inability to change and accomplish it with fresh eyes (and with the motivation of someone who is being followed around figuratively with a gun to the head), **couldn't you achieve your goal if it truly were a matter of life and death for you?**

Now move on to being honest with yourself when it's not a matter of life-and-death, but simply one of differing and competing priorities: Are there goals and needs that keep you from accomplishing what you say you want? You must identify what these are in relation to your goal before you can manage them so that you change the outcome and accomplish your goal.

———◉———

IT'S A GOLDEN AGE FOR MENTAL AND EMOTIONAL HEALTH!

Here is a hopeful thought for you: We are living in what could be described as the golden age for mental and emotional issues. Although let's be clear—it's not that we've solved everything! As a society we don't fully understand all the problems; we can't immediately help all who suffer; and we have to acknowledge that a stigma, when it comes to mental health, still exists. Yet it IS a golden age when compared to any previous time in the history of the world! We already have the ability to help many people; we no longer burn people at the stake for mental issues; we are cracking down on the inhuman warehousing or incarceration of mental patients; we have a robust menu of behavioral techniques that help those challenged by mental issues; and we have a number of safe and effective drugs at our disposal to fight both the chemical causes of mental issues and the consequences they can produce.

Keep in mind that as Dr. James R. Doty pointed out in his book *Into the Magic Shop*, we are just beginning to understand the workings of the brain; it has been studied for only a comparatively brief time from an evolutionary or a medical standpoint. But as we learn more in the future, there will be progress and things will certainly get even better! Today's technology is just beginning to provide tools like FMRI's, MRI's and CAT scans that can give us real insight into what is really going on between our ears and allow us to really study the brain. So no, we are not in utopia yet and things will get even better in the future—but we are moving in that direction, and the situation has never been better. The possibility of making positive emotional and mental changes in our lives has never seemed so likely as it is today!

CHAPTER 2
SNUGGLING WITH DEMONS

"The amount of satisfaction you get from life depends largely on your own ingenuity, self-sufficiency, and resourcefulness."
-William C. Menninger, American scientist, physician, engineer
(1899-1966)

DEMONS AND ZOMBIES of one kind or another are quite popular today in movies and television shows. They also have always been with us in folklore dating back as far as you can go. And as we have established you are in all likelihood a normal but also flawed human being, so it is all but a certainty that you will have one or two of your very own demons by the time you get to adulthood. It's a little bit like:

> **Congratulations on being a member of the human race and on reaching adulthood—now here are your own private demons!!**

What are yours? Possibly you have trouble fully trusting significant others, so your relationships are less fulfilling than you would like. Or maybe you have what feels like uncontrollable bouts of anger or fear? I could go on and on, but the list of demons is too long! The point here is, all of us have them, and those little gremlins sure do bite from time to time! Sometimes they appear singly, but on bad days we may feel like we are battling a small army of them.

This is just another part of being human, unfortunately, and our goal should be to deal with them appropriately.

BUT...WHERE DID THEY COME FROM?

Some people spend their time debating whether our demons come from our upbringing (nurture) or our basic makeup (nature). For some of us, people in our lives who are supposed to love and care for us for some reason simply can't or don't, and this deficiency may create emotional problems or issues for us (nurture). For others of us, we may be genetically programmed (via our biochemistry) to suffer from depression or sadness (nature). The main point is that most of us have negative emotions and demons no matter whether we "invented" them on our own, were born "programmed" with some emotional challenges, or got "help" from family, strangers, acquaintances, peers, or poor role models.

And, while obviously there are some very nasty things that can happen in our upbringing that can create demons, even those who are fortunate enough to have a normal, wholesome upbringing are not immune to having demons. So, I believe the correct answer to the question of whether our demons come from nature or nurture is a resounding, "Yes—both!" The simple fact is virtually no one gets out of childhood unscathed or unencumbered by the little monsters, no matter how great their parents are.

Both positive and negative attitudes and preferences tend to be ingrained early in a child's life, and sometimes the earlier this occurs, the more deeply they are imprinted and the more effort it will take later on to change them. This is true whether they are passed down by the parents or whether a child simply makes his own decision, independent of their parents' influence, about how to survive or thrive in the set of circumstances they face.

DEALING WITH THOSE LITTLE MONSTERS

Since we all have a few demons, it's worth looking into our relationship with them. What do we do with them, and how do we deal with them? It is an unusual relationship because we normally get to choose our relationships (other than for those with family), but our demons do not feel so optional! But even though we do not always realize it or feel we can choose or control our demons, we have a lot more power in this area than most people believe. We are not stuck with our demons...but we still must DEAL with them!

As with other relationships, the key to dealing with our demons is communication and acceptance. Let's deal with communication first.

It is a true blessing and quite wonderful if you have a good friend or significant other with whom you can discuss your demons. Many of us do not do this as much as we should because we tend to try to hide the existence of our demons from others. We may be ashamed of them, or in many cases we may not even be aware of them. For anyone in either of these situations, now is the perfect time to find and benefit from a good therapist if you can do so, along with continuing to read this book! Nothing can be more valuable than the end result of experiencing a peaceful, calm, and productive life, so employ all available options!

It is fair to say that, in general, the more awareness we have about what our precise demons are, and the more acceptance we have in terms of the reality of our relationship with them, the happier and more productive our lives will become. Awareness is knowledge, and acceptance is peace; the two, combined with your decisions concerning what you want to do, can improve your life immeasurably.

So, does this mean that we must ACCEPT our demons? A particularly important first step in being able to successfully manage our demons is to understand and accept whatever characteristics we have if we're going to change their negative influence on our lives. After this step we can go about making changes; but without understanding and accepting the truth, there is little hope for positive change. This is a far cry, however, from saying we must like our demons or live with them forever. What I'm saying is the following:

> **We can certainly modify or change the effect that our demons have on us—but only if we first acknowledge they exist.**

This, my friend, is where acceptance comes in.

WHAT'S THE PROBLEM?

Wonderfully, we don't have to slay our dragons to have our lives magically change! This is fantastic because in many cases, it's not possible to entirely rid ourselves of certain demons; they may be too deeply rooted. This may sound like a bit of really bad luck, but at times this is as good as it gets.

Fortunately, it isn't at all necessary to rid ourselves of them COMPLETELY for our life to improve! We can get most of the benefit just by accepting, acknowledging, challenging, and/or motivating ourselves to deal with them more productively.

To give an example, let's take on the anger demon as our example. Let's say and acknowledge that we are a bit too quick to feel an emotion like anger and stay immersed in it for too long—but simply by knowing this about ourselves, we can change how we ultimately react in the present and for the future! There is a wonderful saying that applies here:

> **"Sometimes I wrestle with my demons, and sometimes we just snuggle."**

To continue with our example, when we realize that we are upset by something someone said or did, we can choose to sit on the couch and indulge in the negative emotions of anger and resentment—and if we take that route, we can sit there being mad until hell freezes over...and nothing will change for the better! But what happens if we understand and accept that we are simply reacting <u>un</u>productively when we do this, and that there is a better way, because we (and others) can grow by affecting change in ourselves? Well then, we might be able to refrain from lashing out at the person who said the upsetting thing to us. We might be able to remain calm and deal with the other person and our current circumstances reasonably, thereby making gains in our lives... and possibly even affecting the lives of others for the better! When we get to the point where we can snuggle with our demons, we've really come a long way toward winning the war.

THE DNA OF DEMONS

Negative emotions and thoughts such as shame, rage, anxiety, and depression are the DNA of our demons. In general, the experience and expression of such emotions is quite varied and not at all uniform among people. People's reactions vary widely and change quickly from person to person. Given the exact same set of experiences, one person may feel fearful, another mad, and another sad or depressed. And yet another individual may simply find the whole situation amusing.

Emotions are not universal in their appearance either. One person who is feeling sad may shed tears while another person may lie down on their couch and have difficulty getting up or doing anything. The same person may have different emotional reactions to the same experience at various times. Finally, the same emotion in two different people may be triggered by totally different events or thoughts.

Naturally, the reactions that people have to their emotions vary widely as well. For example, in some people, the reaction to fear could be anger; in others it might be a need to control their environment in order to avoid the circumstances that created the fear; a third person may just want to go to sleep, and a fourth individual may decide to exercise. Suffice it to say that the reactions are too varied to fully list here.

This all came as news to me; I used to think that if something helped or hurt my peace of mind, it would be that way for others also. But this simply isn't so, and it's why a therapist will want to get a good reading on you and ask you how *you* feel about something you've described before engaging in too much depth about it with you. There are few universal truths about how people think of or react to events, and which emotions arise.

In many cases I believe a given individual's reaction to an event or thought is like water going down a hill. The water hits a rock and either goes left or right due to some minute physical details of the surface that we and others may not be able to discern...or the path is actually being determined by the rotation of the earth. And once a pattern begins, it is more likely to become ingrained. For example, I have been asked several times why I did not get mad during a situation earlier in my life when a caregiver was not meeting my needs. The underlying premise behind the question seemed to be that most people would have gotten mad at the situation. I really can't say why I didn't, except it was not a conscious decision, and that for me sadness and feeling lonely were simply the emotions I felt as the result.

There are two more points about reacting to events or feelings that are important to mention. First, there is what I call "the fear of fear," something with which I believe most people who suffer from panic attacks will understand. Panic attacks are so unpleasant and can come upon a person so quickly that it's hard to avoid being afraid of or living in dread of the next one. Secondly, the terrible feelings associated with panic attacks and other fearful events can also include the reactivation of a previous trauma. I experienced this for myself right before a shoulder operation several years ago when I was strapped down, while awake, on a narrow operating table. It brought back the trauma of being held down by four to five adults when I was about 3-4 years old and needed stitches in my chin after being pushed face-first onto the concrete bottom of a shallow pool. On a scale of 1-10, I'd gauge the reliving of that childhood trauma at a 15 and heading rapidly up to 100! In an instant I was back in my earlier experience as a toddler in what, at this earlier time, was a very scary life-or-death experience. But, as an adult who knew my reaction was unnecessary, I was literally only a fraction of a second away from a possible psychotic break while on that table. Fortunately, a quick-thinking nurse distracted me just long enough to "hit the syringe" and knock me out cold.

I found it remarkably interesting to hear Caroline Myss, a well-known and respected psychologist, acknowledge that even at age fifty she was still trying to get over at least one of her childhood traumas! I have a great deal of empathy for her, and I also find her statement comforting since it reinforces that it is common and normal for all of us to have our negative feelings and thoughts!

It is critically important that you realize how normal and universal it is to have these thoughts and feelings from time to time, rather than beat yourself up and feel you are bad or a failure for having them, or to believe that no one else feels this way.

> **Let go of any guilt and/or shame about having your demons; these negative feelings do no good, and you do not deserve to have them!**

In this regard, we want to be our own best friends and treat ourselves as we would a dear and loving companion. No one in the universe deserves your love and compassion more than you!

CHAPTER 3
MENTAL-HEALTH FOOD GROUPS

LET ME CHANGE GEARS with you for a moment and discuss the USDA's food pyramid, something most of us learned about as kids in school.

If you recall what your teacher once told you, the food pyramid identifies certain nutritional food groups (vegetables, whole grains, lean protein, and so forth) considered the most nutritious for us. These are the food groups which the USDA's experts advise we consume several times a day. Conversely, there are other foods that the USDA recommends we limit; we often classify such foods with such names as processed foods, sweets/candy, junk foods, and so on.

So why bring up the food pyramid? Just as it is with different types of foods, certain emotions and thoughts can be "nutritious" for us, while other emotions and thought patterns we follow can be debilitating and harmful.

When it comes to what are positive thoughts and feelings—for example, joy, peace, and exhilaration—I place them among the mental-health foods that can have a major positive impact on our well-being. Just as it is difficult to truly overdo with veggies and lean protein, it also is difficult to have excessive satisfaction, happiness, love, relaxation, joy, positive attitudes, forgiveness, and good choices in daily life. From a mental point of view, positive emotions such as these comprise the optimum mental-health diet for humanity! As such, we can indulge in these emotions freely.

But a negative mental-health food group also exists. Typical "foods" that would go into that group would be these negative mental-health thoughts and emotions:

Shame Anger Guilt Fear Sadness

Resentment Bitterness Hate Disappointment

Avarice Pride Ego Greed

Sloth Gluttony Depression Blame
Self-hate Regret Jealousy Lust

OBVIOUSLY, THIS LIST could be even longer, but this should give you a good reminder of the negative emotions and feelings we have at times.

These are the emotions and thoughts that pull us down, deplete our motivation and productivity, derail our good intentions, are poor choices, and/or influence us in ways that cause us to feel shame, guilt, or sadness later.

While there isn't a restriction or limit we need to place on our intake of positive mental-health foods, there is one we should have on the intake of negative mental-health foods because we certainly CAN overdo it with these! I think we all can agree that we will experience much more long-term happiness and satisfaction if we limit our experience or intake of negative emotions and feelings just as if they were foods loaded with sugar and saturated trans fats!

But let me have a word of caution here: Back when I first recognized how my intense anxiety was pulling me down, I strove to eliminate all experiences with negative thoughts and emotions. Now I have learned that such a goal is completely:

> Urealistic,
> Impossible, AND
> Unnecessary!

As long as we sample negative thinking and emotions in moderation, they can be fine, and in fact, it is normal for us to have these feelings; they are something we all, as members of the human race, are likely to experience. It is simply the way our brains are wired, and experiencing negative emotions in moderation proves to be a much more realistic goal than a perfectionistic ideal of trying to eliminate them entirely.

Because people who are ensnared by these issues and/or who may have trouble breaking free may also have trouble in the areas set out below:

> Self-confidence or self-esteem

> Ability to both give and receive love
> Trust
> Independence
> Truthfulness
> Intimacy
> Feeling a sense of security or safety daily
> Resentfulness
> Having a positive attitude and outlook on life
> Social interactions
> Ability to delay gratification
> Ability to effectively deal with money
> And many more.

There could be multiple reasons for any one or combination of these issues. What is most important is to find your own demons and deal with them...and don't worry; I won't leave you hanging! Throughout the bulk of this book, you will find how we can do something about the impact that negative thoughts and emotions have on us when they are present.

First, though, we need to go through the work of identifying what troubles or challenges you the most.

———◉———

IDENTIFYING THE HOT BUTTON

Some might argue here that humans are not meant to have mental stability or equilibrium. That's another way of saying that all of us are going to have ups and downs; that's just the way it is. So, anger, frustrations, love and hate, laughter, sadness—they are all part of the deal! If that's the case, then as human beings all we generally might want to do, and all we might be ABLE to do, is to keep it between the lines, by sampling negative emotions only in moderation, and working towards making our daily lives both enjoyable and productive.

So even though we might understand now that it is not possible to avoid feeling negative emotions to at least to some degree from time to time, I do hope we can all agree it is certainly possible to lessen those emotions' severity and frequency. It is for this very reason I want you to look at the negative emotions list at the beginning of this chapter and determine which are most troublesome in your daily living and experiences.

WHAT'S MY PRIMARY NEGATIVE EMOTION?

Certain things about humans are universal: We all want to be nurtured, cared for, loved, appreciated, and accepted. There are also other things or aspects of ourselves and our bodies that are commonplace: Most of us have a dominant hand and eye, for example. And if we spoke to a neurolinguistics practitioner, chances are they would say that we, as humans, all have a dominant sense as well, be it that of touch, smell, hearing, sight, or taste. Doesn't it seem reasonable that at least many of us may have a dominant or primary negative emotion that is pretty much running our lives, despite any previous effort on our part to moderate it?

For instance, with some of us anxiety rules our lives, whereas for others it could be shame, bitterness, guilt, or regret. Or could fear be the root issue?

Whichever it is for you, it is particularly important for you to figure out what your primarily negative emotion is, so you know where to concentrate any self-improvement efforts. You need to be working on the right thought or feeling. First things first; right? Then keep at it!

This is what I began doing as I lived my life. At some point I came to realize that, while I had to deal with depression from time to time, it was never my root issue, and that it was likely that any depression was a result of my failure to control my anxiety and panic attacks. I did not see the value in working primarily on depression; it was not my hot button. That's why I even found it odd when my doctor at the time occasionally prescribed anti-depressant medication for me. Only now do I realize that there is a great deal of overlap in what some medications treat, as well as the common overlap of emotions such as anxiety and depression.

Once I realized what my primary negative emotion was, I began working to overcome this root issue of anxiety/panic attacks ... and over my life I have made very satisfying progress! But to fully understand how a person can change and transform his life, I will give you my history a little later in the book. I hope sharing my story with you will help motivate you and help give you confidence in the process, strategies, and process I advocate.

ORIGINS OF GUILT

While I won't discuss each negative emotion humans experience, I do feel compelled to touch briefly on guilt. I do not think we are born with feelings of guilt (or many of the other aforementioned negative emotions). As far as science has been able to determine, there are no guilt genes in our DNA sequencing. Instead, I am sorry to say we absorb such feelings primarily from our parents and others we encounter early in our life, or we make certain judgements long before we have the experience to do so properly. That is not to say that there are no other sources; but our earliest and most important influences come primarily from our parents, friends, and caregivers and our own assumptions or judgements. These feelings may have been visited upon us by absolutely loving parents with nothing but the best of intentions, but I have always felt that virtually everyone picks up a problem or two during childhood. I am sure there must be exceptions, but my observation is that such exceptions are exceedingly rare.

Here is a short series of statements I feel are unusually pithy and helpful in understanding childhood guilt. They are from the book *Boundaries*, by Dr. Henry Cloud and Dr. John Townsend.

1. Making a child responsible for the feelings of the adult places an unfair burden on the child.
2. If a child feels he is loved when he is "good" and not loved when he is "bad" this is also terrible for the child; it allows for spiritual or emotional extortion; and the child does not get the unconditional love he yearns for.
3. Each of these opens the possibility of using guilt to manipulate the child, which is despicable.
4. While it is necessary to teach a child the difference between acceptable and unacceptable actions, how to disagree appropriately, and how to make corrections, etc., these should not be associated with giving or withholding love from the viewpoint of either the

caregiver or the child.

I was blessed with parents who did not engage in guilting their children, and consequently, I have been relatively free of the destructive power of that influence. On the other hand, I have seen the devastation caused by parents who throw guilt and shame around like a priest dispersing holy water when it comes to their kids. There also are many people who believe that certain religions employ fear, shame, and guilt on an everyday basis even though it isn't part of the formal doctrine. It is not something that is easy for most people to overcome, and the detrimental effects of guilt and shame can devastate a person's entire life. In those cases, and as with the other negative thought or emotional patterns, it behooves the sufferer to work diligently for as long as it takes to overcome these feelings.

Someday I believe we will recognize guilt and shame for what they are: a form of abuse when inflicted by or on others. Of course, we also can be the source of our own guilt, especially when we are young, by making incorrect and/or illogical negative decisions or coming to flawed conclusions. Sadly, this self-imposed guilt can last decades or even a lifetime if not challenged and corrected. For example, as a youngster, I figuratively stamped my little feet and fervently committed to never giving anyone a reason to be disappointed in me for not being perfect. This helped me achieve many transitory goals in my life; but it engendered feelings of guilt when I messed up, making the finding of true relaxation and happiness almost impossible for me to achieve. The earlier we imprint such unrealistic thoughts on our young brains and the more fervently we commit to them, the harsher the consequences are when we inevitably fail to live up to these impossible goals.

You may not complete your work on guilt or any of the other negative emotions the first time you try (I know I certainly did not!), but there are precious few things in life that are more important than making progress toward inner peace and the triumph over the negative thought patterns in our lives. I fully expect to be working on these for the rest of my life, but I do NOT let the fact that I am not yet completely over them pull me down.

If you work diligently, I believe you will experience improvement and more contentment. I am so incredibly grateful for my own progress, and for having a life better than I could have imagined! As of this writing, I spend almost all days happily, in gratitude and joy. The fact that it took many, many iterations to get there is just the way it was for me. If I could have done it sooner or more easily, I would have—but what I do know is I got off of my rear end and gave it all the effort I could while also proceeding to balance other aspects of life, and that was all that I was capable of doing.

As for my early desire to be perfect in all things, I got over the fact that I will never be perfect years and years ago! (But more about that shortly.) I am just happy to continue to work towards increased happiness.

CHAPTER 4

WHY I WENT ON THIS JOURNEY...AND HOPEFULLY, WHY YOU WILL WANT TO AS WELL

LET ME START WITH A very short story. For too long in her life, my mother had severe foot pain and related issues. Purchasing any new pair of shoes was, as a result, always a big and complex deal for my mother due to the intense pain she suffered if she made an incorrect decision. My dad, however, had no similar issues. He could walk into a shoe store, pick out a pair of shoes, and wear them immediately with no worries about potential discomfort. I can clearly remember him saying he "really couldn't understand foot pain" since he didn't have any.

It is very much like this with anxiety issues as well: It can be exceedingly difficult for those who have had no experiences with them to understand or empathize with those who do. And while I am not a trained professional or substitute for one, I have had a good 60+ years of experience with much ultimate success, which I believe puts me in a unique position. I do not have an educational background in either psychology or psychiatry. What I brought to the table in terms of writing this book is six decades of in-depth experience with living 24/7 as a person who has experienced these problems. What comprises the bulk of this book is behavioral and practical tips and strategies versus psychological theory. And while it was not possible to list or discuss all conceivable strategies because circumstances and people differ too widely, those included in this book have an extremely broad application and audience.

In order to learn and come to deal with my issues more effectively versus being at the mercy of them, I've read countless self-improvement books and works on spirituality, and spent innumerable hours in educational courses and group meetings studying different philosophies, learning about the tenants of various religions, overcoming perfection, dealing with my own compulsions, trying to replace many non-productive thinking patterns with positive ones, and participating in life-enriching activities. I have tried and failed **numerous** times, but over time I began to succeed.

I received a BBA followed by an MBA in accounting—but I feel I can speak to my fellow travelers despite this educational background being far afield from that of anxiety issues. As your self-appointed lab rat, I was living with anxiety issues daily, and no single subject in my life has gotten more of my attention!

To combat anxiety's frequent and severe negative influence on my life, I ultimately chose to spend a great deal of time studying and learning methods to resolve both my anxiety and other negative, downward-spiraling emotions like depression. Based upon what I have learned and implemented over my 80-plus years, I can easily say that I am in a more stable, peaceful, and happy state than I ever have been or ever even hoped to be. As of this book's writing I have read about, researched, and uncovered many principles and strategies that bring about progress, satisfaction, and fulfillment in life as well as how to effectively deal with negative issues. These will have an extremely broad application to dealing with nearly *all* anxiety-producing negative emotions like shame, fear, self-blame, jealousy, and more.

My lifelong efforts to deal with my own issues involve what other people might consider to be sacrifices, but that's not how I view them! They were something I was more than willing to do to achieve my personal and professional goals. At this stage of my life, I have left truly little undone that I wanted to do, with very few regrets. Today I enjoy every minute of almost every one of my days due to my feeling of pride and achievement. This is a very gratifying experience!

But not only was I willing to do the work to achieve my goals, but also I realized that it was required, not optional, if I was to reach the goals I had set for myself. As I worked on myself and my goals, I was happy to forgo activities many others might participate in; they simply held no appeal for me. My choices have allowed me to have a rich, exciting, and rewarding journey, and I certainly do not feel like I have lived a sheltered or cloistered life in any way. I have simply made choices that made sense to me and which,

I thought, furthered my goals. (To see some details on my activities and achievements, see Appendix A.)

For me it was the right thing to choose to focus on family, career, exercise, and general health, as well as mental health and spiritual matters. Of course, a different combination of goals might be right for you. None of us really follow the same path and it's up to you to choose for yourself.

Remember, it is NEVER too early to begin and NEVER too late to achieve success! NEVER give in, and NEVER give up! Or as Winston Churchill is famous for saying, "Never, never, never quit!"

BEGINNINGS

Let me briefly go back in time to show you what prompted me to begin my journey.

I was born tongue-tied, something I believe could be the start of my anxiety issues as a young child. I had a lot of trouble making myself understood! I recall being very annoyed and exasperated that no one could follow what I said when I attempted to speak, and while my tongue-tied condition was eventually corrected, there were feelings of frustration and anxiety that started as a direct result of the condition. Overall, though, I had a healthy childhood, with a generally healthy constitution.

I also believe that experiencing what I consider to be more than my fair share of anxiety was also caused by not being able to get the security and warm fuzzies I longed for at key points as a child. I was anxious and wanted warmth, love, care, and hugs. When I went to my mother and woke her up in the middle of the night to get some of what I wanted so badly, it turned out to be traumatic for both of us, due to her reaction upon being awakened. Without going into specifics, my mother later told me when I was in my 20's that her reactions stemmed from having been abused as a child. But as a result, I was unable to shake my anxiety and it grew and grew.

Another major contributing factor to my anxiety issues had to do with trying to be a perfectionist, something I've mentioned in the previous chapter. This was an unsustainable and unhealthy approach to life and its circumstances, and perfection grew only more difficult to achieve as I aged and the various demands from different areas of my life —my marriage, career, family, children, social, spiritual life, etc.—became more important, varied, and pressing. These are the facets of life which hopefully would provide good feelings and comfort; but since I was pursuing them from the point of view that I would only be happy if I did everything PERFECTLY in each of these areas, there was no real hope of my experiencing peace or relaxation on a sustained basis!

And to put a cherry on top of the mental quagmire I constructed for myself by trying to be perfect, I also indulged in the full blown "Atta boy, aww s@#*" components when I failed. Upon the occurrence of any mistake, all my previous atta boys! or congratulations and accomplishments seemed to vanish instantaneously and forever from my mind. This abrupt 180-degree change in my thoughts about myself, my prior achievements, and my accomplishments pretty much assured that not only would I have no real chance of meeting the impossible perfection goal I set for myself, but also that I was building an internal mechanism to severely beat myself up every single time I failed. I was a very harsh critic of myself and felt all was lost anytime there was even a minor or normal variance from my impossible goal.

Finally, at age 65 I discovered I had severe sleep apnea. How long it may have existed before being diagnosed is anyone's guess at this point, but I feel certain that this was a contributor to at least some of the significant panic attacks I experienced. For example, many times I experienced being very relaxed and feeling fine at night, only to doze off and then awake with a start, gasping for breath, with my heart pounding.

I am aware that sleep apnea certainly does not lead to panic attacks for everyone. But in my case, I was already primed for anxiety issues, so this sudden and inexplicable nighttime gasping for air that was combined with a racing heart was more than sufficient to scare the bejesus out of me and ensure a good panic attack on top of the sleep apnea!

Google tells us that sleep apnea was first diagnosed in the mid 1960's. I was in my 20's at that point and just beginning to seriously work on my issues. Since I am still polishing and refining, I can only wish fervently that someone had put the 2 issues together sooner. Actually, I was the first to connect these two for my situation, despite my explaining numerous times to at least one psychiatrist and one behavioral psychologist exactly what was happening. I can honestly say that I hold no hard feelings concerning this, however; they were excellent therapists, they helped me in many other ways, and I am confident they were doing their level best. And no one is perfect.

Not surprisingly, with so many avenues available to me to experience anxiety and panic attacks, including my fear of fear, I experienced disappointment, frustration, and sadness during all too many days. As a devout perfectionist, I let any errors or failures on my part cause severe declines in my self-image, with increases in frustration, anxiety, and hopelessness. All too often, I entered a fairly deep depression from which I would have to extricate myself. I was the embodiment of my friend Sisyphus, pushing his rock up the mountain daily, only to have to begin again the next day.

GENETICS AND MEDICATION

There was more that may have contributed to my experiences of anxiety than I've just detailed, however. I discovered I had some brain chemistry and possibly other hereditary issues that contributed. You see, my dad also suffered from anxiety and depression.

It is amazing to me what problems a small, unchecked, and abnormal amount of one or more of a person's brain chemicals can cause! I have no knowledge of the specific chemicals involved, but I stubbornly resisted taking the medication I needed to put everything back to normal. Although I dislike pain and suffering as much as anyone, at the time I was trying to please all the stakeholders in my life who were giving me conflicting advice. I refrained from taking the medicine because I didn't want to offend anyone, and because I was afraid of becoming addicted and dying. I hasten at light speed to assure readers that my resistance to medication was unfounded, unsupported by facts, and irrational! It inflicted decades of pain and suffering on me, and by attribution, on my family.

If you might be wondering as to why I let this go on for so long, suffice it to say that I have always been able to endure pain very well, and I always have been willing to endure almost anything for the sake of achieving my goals, whether professional or personal. Obviously, a choice like this has both positive and negative consequences; and what is true of me is that I am focused more on my goals rather than the effort or pain involved in the achievement of those goals. Of course, this is lovely if you genuinely want to achieve your goals, but it has some obvious flaws if you value comfort and peace.

While some may consider my tolerance of pain to be somewhat bizarre, it's a trait I share with my brother. For example, when we were young, my brother and I decided to adopt an unusual method of remembering to practice good oral hygiene. For some reason we mutually decided that the way to really ensure our remembering this was to totally forego the use of pain-killing shots during dental work done for cavities and such. To this day I have clear memories of sitting in a chair while the dentist drilled away (and this was before the use of the better high-speed drills available today) and either squeezing metal balls or gripping tightly the arms of the chair to get through the pain of the procedure. By the time the ordeal was over, I would be drenched in sweat and totally exhausted. But it was a pact that I had made with my big brother, and I was not about to wimp out!

This went on every six months for a four-to-five-year period, and while it worked to keep me brushing to the highest level possible, I must say it was excruciating when drilling was needed. But I was willing to endure the pain to achieve the goal.

⎯⎯⎯◉⎯⎯⎯

SUMMING UP THE CAUSES AND EFFECTS

If you are still having some difficulty understanding why anxiety and panic attacks would create so much lifelong frustration and pain for me, let me just explain it this way: Imagine that you feel your entire life, all your work to date, your happiness, your hopes, your dreams, and your goals in the future are all totally dependent on your performance—but you also realize that YOU are the one sabotaging your own performance with anxiety and panic attacks that you are powerless to control. That's how I felt for 40 years, so no wonder self-improvement directed at this part of my life became one of my main focuses! Almost every day I was either working to resolve and overcome the last attack and/or worrying about the occurrence of the next one. And I only made it worse by layering on top of my perfectionistic outlook the atta boy, aww s@#* kicker anytime I deemed myself to have fallen short of my own unrealistic expectations.

> **I realized that I was doing it to myself—this was incredibly frustrating!**

Looking back now, I can hardly conceive of a more complete combination of unfortunate mental and physical symptoms to ensure ongoing incidences of stress, excessive anxiety, and depression. Yet I know there are others with far worse situations, and it is the hope of helping them that motivates me to continue my book.

I do hope my life story and experience help illustrate that the roots of an individual's anxiety, pain, despair, depression, shame, or panic patterns can be complex, and that they can be caused by any combination of the following:

> Nature and/or nurture: heredity, DNA, upbringing, and/or environment

> The workings of the brain: over- or under-activity in certain portions of the brain

> Chemical and hormone imbalances

> Personality types

> Not achieving emotional balance when young

> A very wide variety of possible job stresses

> Unreasonable fears

> Other medical conditions (such as sleep apnea or being tongue-tied)

> Inappropriate (but unchecked) decisions made when people are too young to be aware of their possible negative consequences.

This is only a recounting of the specific issues that affected me directly or indirectly. Only God and seasoned mental health professionals know the full list for others, many of which can be TOUGH to unearth, deal with, and correct.

And as to how they affected me, let me briefly cite some of the major day-to-day issues I created for myself or simply endured. I hope none of these will be familiar to you:

> A fair amount of concern about the physical effects of the stress and anxiety I have experienced and what this may have done to me and the toll it may have taken on my body over fifty to sixty years. I am grateful, and in awe to some degree, that no terrible effects have surfaced. The human body and its ability to adapt and survive amazes me.

> Not being as spontaneous and fun to be with as I might otherwise be.

> Difficulty with relaxing and enjoying normal activities.

> Conducting way too many business meetings during which I had sweat literally dripping off my face due to my anxiety.

> Attended any number of New Orleans Saints games during which I excessively worried about what was coming up Monday at work. I often got nauseous because of this, and my focus was more on calming myself and not throwing up than enjoying the game and the people I was sharing it with.

> There also were days at work when I would run the 10 flights of stairs in our office building to try to get rid of excess anxiety and energy. I tried anything and everything I could think of to try to rid myself of nervous energy and relax.

> Countless nights during which my anxiety level was so high that I could not get a decent night's sleep. My mind would race at

1,000 miles a minute with my pulse pounding. I often got in the trap of "I need to go to sleep to be rested for work, to do well, avoid mistakes, and achieve my long-term career goals. But when I get in bed, my anxiety gets worse. But I need to sleep..." And then my mind would spin even faster! As I was afraid this reaction would kill me, I would go out to walk or run at 3 or 4 AM just to completely wear myself out and get rid of the nervous energy so I could get some sleep.

› Numerous minor and full-blown panic attacks. These were very unpleasant and scary. They could begin in a split second, and I felt I could go from being comfortable to being in a state of extremely high anxiety in less than a full second.

› During a full-blown panic attack, I would be totally debilitated and unable to function. I couldn't think rationally or logically or even make the most basic of decisions such as whether to eat, what to eat, whether I should "risk" having a sip or two of water, what to do, and whether to even sit or stand. I was extremely fearful and felt as though I had totally lost control of my mind.

———◦———

PICTURE THIS

Here's an accurate picture of the depths to which my perfection affected me: For roughly 35 years, if I were to make a mistake or not know the answer to almost any question, most often I would blush, start to sweat (profusely), immediately shut down internally, outwardly go silent, and then mentally, and sometimes physically, beat the crap out of myself for what I perceived as a profound shortcoming. All too often, the upset I experienced stayed with me for days or weeks and dominated ALL OF my thoughts and actions! Frequently I would go into a mild or severe depression for a brief time because of my internal anxiety.

Yet because I was still able to perform well in my professional life by sheer force of will, I was always promoted quickly to increasing levels of responsibility. Unfortunately, this had some adverse effects on me, as I had not received sufficient time to assimilate and grow comfortably and of course, I made mistakes, as any employee does in a new position. I often found myself supervising others in their performance of functions I had never performed myself, which led to additional stress, fears of inadequacy, and an imposter syndrome which intruded periodically into my professional life.

So how did I react? I continued to do the best I could, and while from outward appearances I was quite successful, rarely was I comfortable or at peace.

RISING ABOVE

From all I've recounted earlier in this chapter, I can imagine that a person who does not know me at all might well assume that my life turned out to be a total and absolute disaster! But I was fortunate that, partly by sheer force of will, partly by a lot of help from certain loving and caring individuals, and partly by reading about, researching, and developing ways to combat anxiety, depression, and their related fallout, I was able to achieve my own salvation! Again, see Appendix A if you are interested in more specifics about my life.

I tried out certain strategies and practices. I would try and fail; try again and fail, and try again and fail again. Yet I never gave up and ultimately succeeded. I fought my way through all of it and today enjoy a glorious life filled with a wonderful family and accomplishments of which I will always be proud! I have had two incredible wives (separately, thank you), four of the most wonderful children a person could ever hope for, loving parents, a great brother, fantastic athletic coaches, inspiring teachers, and an educational and professional life filled with successes and accomplishments from junior high school forward.

Self-improvement has now become a near life-long hobby of mine and rarely does a day go by that I am not trying to do something to improve myself. Some people strive for bigger, faster, stronger. I try to be better, happier, and more relaxed!

I have few if any self-destructive behaviors now, and I am quite happy to work on areas that I see as having potential for my growth. I am certainly not perfect, but I am at peace with myself to a degree I could not imagine earlier in my life. For the most part I have avoided excess anxiety by understanding its roots, and working towards, and becoming more aware of how I affect others. Also, I've made great strides replacing the anger, expectations, and the frustration I previously directed towards myself with non-judgmental acceptance of my own deficiencies and shortcomings. Of course, I have also used the ideas, principles, and strategies in this book as well. I have done a major makeover on myself and am quite satisfied with who I am these days. For me this is huge!

I still have what used to be anxiety-triggering thoughts every single day, on the trips I take, on many nights just when I am going to sleep, and at times when I am alone. However, now I just look at them and let them go, knowing they are just thoughts my reptilian brain coughs up like hairballs and that I am not at the effect or mercy of them any longer. They have little or no charge left in that they no longer send me spiraling into anxiety or depression. I know I can manage them, so they have no power. They truly are like clouds that just float by. I am at times a little sad that I had to endure my issues; but I am grateful that they are effectively behind me, and I am excited about things I can do now.

I feel like Lou Gehrig without the disease—the luckiest man in the world! And as I want you to achieve this same kind of joy more quickly than I did and with the smallest possible fraction of the pain, I have identified in this book many different ideas, principles, and strategies helpful in combatting, minimizing and/or overcoming negative emotions and feelings. Also, there are numerous statements, facts and opinions that may help. It is particularly important to have as many ways as possible to train or redirect your mind and keep your thoughts and feelings in balance, at peace, and working towards your goals. The term "different strokes for different folks" applies here, as different strategies work for different problems, different mindsets, and different times. And that's good news. No matter what your particular or unique issues or thoughts and emotions are...

> **The more strategies you have at hand, the more arrows in your quiver, the better and the higher your**

chance is of being successful with fighting those demons!

As we say in New Orleans: Variety is mo' betta!

PREVENTIVE MEASURES

As you begin to put the principles and strategies into practice in your life, keep this particularly key point in mind: Almost all these ideas work best before the occurrence of a full-fledged anxiety attack or depressive episode, etc. In other words, it is always preferable to do the work up front and thereby reduce or avoid the problem if you can.

It's like what we try to do with our physical health by going in for annual wellness check-ups, and not just waiting until something seems wrong. Doing this with your mental and emotional health can be the difference between feeling normal or even like being king of the world vs. feeling like a failure, abnormal, and out of control.

If you like images, think of it this way: It is always easier to keep a train moving in the right direction than it is to get it started from a static position or to stop it and turn it around once it gets up a full head of steam and is charging down the tracks in the wrong direction.

> **DO THE WORK UP FRONT; IT'S IMPORTANT!!!**

FINAL THOUGHTS

The good news is that progress only takes a willingness and commitment to try and to keep trying. It is best to accept the possibility that failures will occur; this can make it easier to continue to risk, to try, and to take the initiative. Mistakes may occur, setbacks may well happen, and not everything goes perfectly even after you understand mentally what the cause is and what the best course of action may be.

It is up to each of us to make our decisions – they cannot be avoided, since "no decision" is a decision as well. Just remember, it is never too late to do any of the following:

> Change and improve yourself.
> Learn, grow, find more peace.
> Treat yourself and others with more love and respect.
> Demand that you be treated with more respect by others.
> Improve your life.
> Lose weight.
> Increase your exercise.
> Be involved with multiple other activities.

And if it is never too late for the above, then the corollary is...

> IT IS ALWAYS TOO SOON TO STOP TRYING!

Give it some thought.

"The purpose of life is not to be happy. It is to be useful, to be honorable, to be compassionate, to have it make some difference that you have lived and lived well."

- Ralph Waldo Emerson

If you do agree that this is at least an aspirational idea, you might also agree that, to live up to your potential and come as close as you can to achieving this purpose, you need to be as fully functioning as possible. And this is only possible when you shed your unproductive thought patterns. So let's get to it!

PART II

LAWS OF THE UNIVERSE
OR "LOU'S"

PART II - OVERVIEW

I ORIGINALLY BEGAN thinking about this book just in terms of trying to set forth all the specific strategies I have used to combat pain and anxiety, but it became apparent to me over time that there are some overarching principles which we need to accept in order to get to the maximum level of peace, calm, joy, and productivity in life.

These principles can be referred to as **LOU'S, or Laws of the Universe,** but for those more spiritually inclined, you can refer to them as GHT's .... God's Honest Truths. These are foundational principles for starting the work of dealing with stress, depression, shame, anxiety, and other negative emotions or thoughts.

Because they are more general and foundational than the specific strategies that follow, I want to begin with the LOU'S. The important distinctions I would make between LOU'S and strategies are the following:

> LOU'S are general mindsets (e.g., being willing to accept delayed gratification). The strategies are specific (e.g., exercising).

> While your practice and acceptance of LOU'S should generally include the whole group, it is fine to accept or reject the specific strategies based on your personal preferences. Naturally, you may not have the same level of effectiveness and use across all the LOU'S, but a rejection of any of these principles, or an ignoring of them, can negatively affect what you hope to achieve.

> And while I will advise you later not to try to implement or even employ all strategies at first, I feel your overall success will be enhanced the more and the sooner you can embrace all LOU'S. If, at first, you find you cannot embrace a LOU, I would suggest that

you give it serious thought and at least keep an open mind about
it rather than rejecting it.

CHAPTER 5

WE ARE THE PRODUCT OF OUR CHOICES

FROM THE MINUTE WE are born until the minute we die, we all strive to control our environment. This is not entirely possible to do, of course, but most of us have the innate desire to try.

Fortunately, the universe in which we live provides us with one extremely powerful lever that we may use to bend the course of the universe in the direction we prefer. This is CHOICE! We make choices 24/7/365, literally; and it is no exaggeration to say that we are the product of our choices.

OH, THE CHOICES WE MAKE!

Those choices we make are for the most part entirely up to us; and the results we have in life, as well as the control we achieve over life, are a result of the choices we make.

Happily, much of the time the universe leaves us alone to pursue those choices. However, at times the universe may decide that something is going to happen, and no matter what you may do about it, the universe is undeterred. For example, if nature or the universe decides that a class-five hurricane will hit your particular coastline, you are not going to have a delightful day at the beach no matter how much you may work at or wish for it.

Yet on the other hand, there is normally a huge amount of flexibility in the universe that allows you to use choice to gain control of your life most of the time. In fact, the universe really doesn't care a whole lot about a huge percentage of our daily lives! Whether we are happy, successful, well-educated, etc. is left up to us.

But even though the universe does not care what we do, we do! And we can be successful by making the proper choices.

———⊙———

CAPTAINS OF OUR FATE

Many people believe themselves to be simply pawns of chance and fate, and that's a philosophy with which I do not agree! I acknowledge there are some things we cannot change no matter how much we try (e.g., I will never be 6 feet 2 inches tall or run a 4-minute mile), but I definitely agree with the folks who say we are captains of our fate to a large degree.

Almost everything we do in life is a choice. It might help to think about it this way: Do you get out of bed in the morning? If so, when? What do you eat each day? Do you exercise or not? Are you in a dead-end job or relationship that needs to be changed? Do you choose to go in for a checkup when you feel something funny is going on with your body, or do you decide to tough it out? Do you try to further your personal goals in your downtime, or do you prefer to just watch television or videos? Do you choose to eat nutritiously or not? Do you overindulge in drugs and alcohol? Do you help other people or turn away? You are making decisions every moment of your life; and the list of the choices you make is certainly exceedingly long. Yet the list of all possible choices is effectively infinite.

Importantly, if you consistently choose to have a better life for your family and work towards that end, you are likely to achieve it if you live in a country where freedom of choice is honored. Achieving happiness, making money (and these two are not the same!), getting a good education, and almost all of the other goals most of us have are within our grasp and can be achieved if we make the appropriate choices and commit ourselves to doing the necessary work.

Appropriate choice may be the only lever you need to apply to achieve your goals. That is good news! However, this is one of those notable examples of something being simple yet difficult at the same time. The importance of choice is quite simple to grasp—but adopting, refining, and perfecting this concept in our daily lives is quite the challenge. It is truly the work of a lifetime for each of us.

UNIFYING PRINCIPLE OF LIFE

Here is another way to look at the importance of choice. My understanding is that physicists are trying extremely hard to develop the unifying principle that reconciles all known individual laws of normal as well as quantum physics (whatever the heck they may be!). The scientists haven't worked this out quite yet, but in all fairness, their problem is tough. Yet we might ask a similar question: What is the unifying principle of life? For me, the unifying principle of life is CHOICE. Give this condensed explanation some thought:

> › CHOICES DETERMINE OUR DECISIONS
> › DECISIONS DETERMINE OUR TIME MANAGEMENT
> › TIME MANAGEMENT DETERMINES OUR LIFE!

These equivalences are valid. Watch your choices and decisions; they control how you spend your time and where you put your efforts and therefore your life and all you will ever be, do, or have.

So be sure your choices support your deepest desires and aspirations. Choices are all we have in life, and the choices we make decide almost every aspect of our lives.

PATTERNS AND EFFORTS

Here is a slightly expanded way to look at the situation, but you can easily merge the two:

> › Choices lead to thoughts
> › Thoughts lead to words
> › Words lead to actions
> › Actions lead to habits
> › Habits lead to character and personality
> › Character and personality lead to destiny

This process goes on in our lives 24/7/365, and I do not feel this is hyperbole. As I mentioned previously, even a failure to choose is a choice—and so the pattern just mentioned will continue! It NEVER stops. And thus, it is to our own benefit to actively take part in this process and work toward our goals.

CHOICES MAKE OUR DESTINY

In line with this: It is always best to think carefully about our choices BEFORE we speak or act on them, because the natural progression AFTER we make our choices will result in our destiny, as shown in the list above. Thus, it behooves us all to look carefully at those decisions we make and directions we head in, even though this sometimes happens when we are too young to remotely grasp the full implications or understand the consequences. Thankfully, though, we can make changes later in life if needed. But ultimately our thoughts, emotions, words, actions, and habits are only CHOICES, so they can be CHANGED! It just takes some effort and persistence on our parts.

As we've discussed:

> **You are responsible for your own life! You control what you become, and YOU have the power to make positive changes in almost all areas.**

Remember that:

> Every action you take is a choice you make;

> Each strategy you may use to accomplish anything in life is a choice you make;

> Each wise or unwise statement you make is a choice;

> Your very thoughts are a choice;

> And the arc and final outcome of your life are very much determined by your...CHOICES!!

SEEING WHAT'S RIGHT BEFORE US

A final critical point is that most of us have many more choices in our lives than we tend to recognize, especially when we are anxious or depressed. I know for myself that when anxious, my physical vision actually narrows and my mind often does not see all options. When we are in a panic, rage, or other painful episode of any variety, we do not understand or see clearly all the possibilities that exist for us. For me, this is an excellent reason not to hurry major decisions.

THE GREATEST MIRACLE!

Many people have a favorite book, and *The Greatest Miracle* by Og Mandino (TGM) happens to be mine. I read the entire book two or three times and a particular section of it well over 100 times. (The reason for doing this is set out in Og's book; and in terms of making new habits and ingraining thoughts into your daily actions, nothing takes the place of REPETITION!)

I am so impressed by this book that I have purchased and given away at least 50 copies to various friends who I thought might benefit from its concepts. I am such a big proponent because I honestly believe it can cause a positive change in a person's life rather quickly. The more you think of and live by the five amazingly simple principles set forth in the book, the happier and more productive I believe your life will become.

Introducing you, the reader, to this book is one of the biggest gifts I can provide. The book's five basic principles are as follows:

1. Count your blessings
2. Proclaim your rarity
3. Go the extra mile
4. Use wisely your power of choice
5. Do all things with love, for yourself, for others, and for God.

Virtually everyone can benefit from being aware of, and trying to adhere to, these principles; and everyone can achieve a richer and fuller life by doing so.

I was so impressed by the usefulness of these principles that I went back to the book at one time to determine whether the myriad ideas presented during a series of group therapy sessions on weight control could be included within the five principles presented in TGM. I was excited to see that, in fact, they could. Then I did the same thing with my group of 25 affirmations I was using at the time, and I found that all of my affirmations also fit within the five principles explained in TGM. Finally, and quite significantly, it dawned on me that the first three and the last principle are really subsets of the fourth: CHOICE!

That was about as close to a "Eureka!" moment as I will probably ever experience. The revelation brought home quite clearly to me the importance of choice in our lives. It is also why I consider choice to be the first LOU.

CHOICE AND ANXIETY

Since anxiety is my primary negative emotion, let me discuss how it can affect the ability to choose. Then I will go on to discuss choice and a broader grouping of negative emotions and thoughts.

It is intuitive that when the anxious mind sees fewer choices than truly exist, it often can intensify the level of anxiety a person feels. Many of those options would reduce the anxiety, but we do not recognize they are available to us! This might help explain why at times a bout of anxiety can spiral out of control. To a large degree I believe that the number of options we see is inversely related to the seriousness of an anxiety attack.

A corollary to this discussion is the following:

> **The more options we think we have, the less anxious we are.**

And remember, just because you may not be able to access or recognize the choices available does not mean there are none. In the throes of a serious anxiety attack I know that my reasoning powers are limited, and so I can never think of all the options I might easily recognize if I were more relaxed and in a more normal state of mind.

I would be remiss if I did not mention that age and the acquiring of wisdom or good judgment also has a lot to do with understanding our available choices, but it's a process that can be difficult to speed up in our lives. To paraphrase one definition of good judgment, it comes from experience...and experience comes from poor judgment! But while this may be true for most of us too much of the time, don't you agree that it is better to read about, and possibly get, the lesson in a much less painful and effortless way?

CHOICE AND OUR EMOTIONS

To an extent, we choose all the feelings and emotions we have. That is a rather large and controversial statement, and I understand why: When I used to suffer greatly from anxiety, I did not think I had the tools needed to effectively combat those feelings. Had you told me back then that it was my choice to feel as I did, I would have vehemently argued the point! So perhaps I might choose to reword the statement as follows:

> **To an exceptionally large degree, humans can choose the feelings they experience, but often we do not have sufficiently developed tools to enjoy and take advantage of this!**

I believe that how a person feels is largely a choice because there are so many options before us to feel otherwise! Possibly all the options are not available to each of us at all times, but if and when that's the case, they can be learned! We simply must do the work to acquire the missing skills, so we have the maximum number of available choices. That is why, eventually, it is possible for many of our feelings to be ones we choose.

If you happen to disagree with me here, let me offer proof that to a large degree, feelings are a choice. The fact of the matter is, not everyone reacts the same way to the exact same situation, as mentioned above:

> Some may laugh when others cry.
> Some people get angry while others get sad.

And perhaps there were even times when you have said to yourself, "I really wish I could feel like they do about this!" When faced with a calamity, one person may be able to count their blessings while another becomes anxious, fearful, angry, or depressed.

I could go on and on, but I believe a person can alter how he perceives things and how he reacts to them. I believe this because I have done it myself and reaped incredible benefits from doing so. Furthermore, I believe that you too can do the exact same thing! It is a long-term choice as to whether you wish to hold on to the debilitating effects of hurts, regrets, anger, shame, guilt, sorrow, sadness, etc., or find a way to let them go. You have a HUGE say in whether your life will be happy and peaceful, or not.

A quite simple example of this is whether you decide to look at events from an optimistic or a pessimistic viewpoint. Either of these mindsets or attitudes will have a huge effect on all aspects of your life.

In short, through the power we already have or can develop to discern our choices, we have a tremendous amount of control over our lives and whether we will be happy and productive.

———◦———

THE IMPORTANT QUESTION

So, the important question for anyone who is suffering is:

> **What are you doing to IMPROVE the situation? What do you have on tap for today that is more important than learning to overcome your unwanted or terrible feelings? What are you CHOOSING to do about them?**

I realize that your head may go crazy when you read that much of life, including your actions and feelings, is your choice; my head certainly did so once upon a time! But with time and thought you should be able to perceive this LOU more clearly.

Also, please be clear that your choices include both your mental state—what you think about—as well as your actions—what you do.

—————◆—————

THE ENEMY

We have all seen and heard people who profess that they are willing to do anything to accomplish a given objective. Yet the goal that they say they are trying to achieve never comes about! Now while I have a tremendous amount of empathy for these people (having been there myself and continuing to visit this place occasionally), as Walt Kelly's cartoon character Pogo said:

> ## "WE HAVE MET THE ENEMY, AND HE IS US!"

For example, I have done this very thing—failed to achieve my objective, despite saying I would do whatever it takes—when it came to my goal of losing and controlling my weight at various times in my life. I must own up to continuing to make poor eating choices at times. I know WHAT to do, and I could do the correct thing! There is no food goblin that comes into the house at night, ties me down, and force-feeds me. Nope, I am the one making the bad choices! This, despite the fact that I had taken the time to type over seven pages of reasons as to why losing weight is a matter of life and death and why it totally affects a person's quality of life, and after I put together another seven-plus pages of notes on how to accomplish my desired weight loss. Yet I have literally and figuratively discussed this material while eating ice cream and cake! I wasn't saying what I really wanted; I was simply lying to myself and others. If I actually wanted to lose weight as much as I said, I could have and would have made it happen.

Most often we want to blame others or circumstances for our shortcomings when, in fact, we ourselves are the true culprits...the enemy among us! So, I now have stopped talking about what I want to do about my weight, as it is more accurate and truthful to simply look at what I am doing and the choices I am making to see what it is that I genuinely want in this area.

IT'S UP TO YOU!

The wonderful thing about seeing options is that you feel empowered. You have a choice; you can change the way you feel or react to certain circumstances over time; and you are not locked into negative, disruptive, or harmful patterns. But what is needed is for you to really want to change and be willing to work at it.

Having this burden or responsibility on our shoulders is a little scary at first. It can be so much easier to blame other people or circumstances for not achieving a desired goal. But a big part of growing up is taking responsibility for our own actions—and it feels good to know it is up to us, and that in most cases no one and no force exists in the universe that can stop us!

It may take time to acquire the necessary skills, to be able to see the choices before us, and finally to exercise our power of choice. But please believe that the mental health chronicles are replete with examples of individuals performing herculean feats in this regard...and you can do the same!

THE PHASES OF CHOICE

Most of us go through three phases in recognizing and availing ourselves of choices:

> Phase 1. We feel there are no choices. Things are as they are, or we simply must do the one thing or option we see before us in a given set of circumstances. It is extremely important at times like these to remember to look for options, especially when we do not see any!

> Phase 2. We acknowledge that, in fact, some choices may exist, but feel INCAPABLE of accessing or using them. In this case, we must continue to reach out; to try to take the next step and continue to look for options we feel we can adopt.

> Phase 3. We finally get to the point (hopefully!) where we can both SEE and EXERCISE our ability to make good choices. Knowing is not sufficient; we must, to quote Nike:

- **JUST DO IT!**

⎯⎯◆⎯⎯

TENNIS ANYONE?

To further illustrate how choices at first may seem not even to exist but eventually become part of our reality, please allow me to use the analogy of a tennis player.

A person starting to play tennis is very inexperienced! They do not really have any choice as to which shot to take in each situation; the best that they do at this stage of learning the game is to simply return the ball over the net and within the boundary lines. They don't know about all the possible shots to take, and generally don't have the skill to make a winning shot.

If a wiser and experienced player were to suggest to this novice that they work on their shot selection, the novice would likely laugh and look at the experienced player like they had two heads. However, after playing for a while and possibly even taking lessons, that novice can come to understand more about the various shot options and begin to realize the best shot in a situation even if they cannot actually make it. Eventually though, with more practice and lessons, they begin to be able to make better shots. Ultimately, they can identify and develop the ability to execute the different shots properly.

The more experienced player may even get a coach, trainer, and nutritionist; but the one thing that all good players do is...practice, practice, practice! Even those at the professional level work relentlessly on their game and their shots. They know they cannot sit on their haunches and expect to be successful. They keep at it for their entire tennis career.

Here is a reasonably complete list of the skills that strong tennis players must master:

> Forehand

> Backhand

> Slice forehand and backhand

> Overhead

> Serves: spin, slice, flat, ace, change of pace

> Return of serve (coming at you at over 130 mph in some cases)

> Serve and volley

> Volley

> Lob

> Passing shots

> Drop shot

> Hitting at different speeds (pace)

> Staying on the base line

> Charging the net

> Running around your backhand

> Wrong-footing your opponent

> Different grips, or ways to hold and use your racquet

> Serving into the opponent's body or away from him or her

> Top spin

> Back spin

But for tennis, as it is in life, there are many other factors to contend with. For

example:

- Guard against unforced errors.
- Deal with bad calls at times and keep playing at your highest level.
- Learn the rules of the games in order to succeed.
- Avoid service faults, double faults, foot faults.
- Know when to use each shot.
- Scout your opponents.
- Play with an injury.
- Deal with tough competition, even when you may not feel like it.
- Deal with your opponents trying to psych you out.
- Learn various strategies for singles and/or doubles tennis.
- Learn how to keep score, and what really matters.

Now think about something: As complex as all this may seem, tennis is really a fairly simple game! Life in total is infinitely more complex and you play it all day, every day, at breakneck speed with no letups at all! And the complexities are such that they can never be fully mastered.

Tennis is very analogous—on some levels—to going through life and learning to make correct decisions. We do not start out with the ability to make the right decision, but with practice, experience, and possibly some coaching, various options which were previously unavailable to us become apparent; and we can choose wisely to further our own proficiency. With knowledge and experience we learn to employ more appropriately all the nuances that an infinite variety of situations demand. We become an expert on our own life and increasingly master and employ the freedom of choice available to us 24/7/365.

The subsequent pictures of this excellent and impactful sculpture highlight the phases of levels of choice we've discussed. We spend our lives going from left to right through the stages shown. To a degree, the picture below shows both four points along the path to mastering tennis ... or life.

FROM A DIFFERENT VIEW, it looks like this

—

———⊙———

SO, MY FRIEND, THERE is no reason for hopelessness or a feeling of helplessness! Feeling that we do not have choices is generally a lie we all too often tell ourselves to avoid taking responsibility or a sign that we are lacking certain skills. Don't let this be characteristic of the way you live your life!

You might look at the sculpture as a metaphor for life. How far towards the right would you like to move? How much effort are you willing to devote to this? There is no one answer for everyone, but these are among the most important decisions you will ever make.

———⊙———

BUT I'VE ALWAYS DONE IT THIS WAY...IT'S JUST THE WAY I AM!

The English author C. S. Lewis (1898-1963) once said: "An explanation of cause is not a justification by reason." Let's think about this for a moment when it comes to the topic of choice. We likely all know people who, when they make a bad choice or do something wrong, say something to the effect of, "I did ____ because ______." That may be fine, for example, if they fill the second blank with something like, "It is the right thing to do." But if a person fills it with something similar to, "I have always done it that way," or even, "I have a thing about that," it might be time to reevaluate the choice being made. Perhaps that person needs to make a change, find a different plan of action, or walk to the beat of a different drummer. In other words:

> **Open yourself up to changing your choices rather than simply justifying your current pattern of action, and remaining stagnant when there is an opportunity for positive change.**

For instance, I made a choice to seize an opportunity that was before me when I was making a list of affirmations and things I wanted to experience in life. I included one that said, "I really enjoy being out of town." At the time, that was anything but true! I had experienced some of the worst times of my life while out of town—so my affirmation was what I HOPED to be able to achieve, and not the life I was living. It was so far from my reality that each time I reviewed that particular affirmation in my head I chuckled at its absurdity. I had zero evidence indicating it would really happen; and initially, I certainly did not feel that I had any choice in the matter. I simply longed for it to be the case and soldiered on.

As the years went by and I have been able to see, and then make, the correct choices for myself, that affirmation about enjoying myself when out of town became true and became my reality! Now when I think of or repeat that affirmation, it is not only a confirming positive statement about travelling (rather than just being a wish), but also a source of considerable pride that reaffirms the progress I have made in terms of my happiness and self-improvement.

If you too decide to move forward in the direction of change for the better in terms of what was once status quo for you, how do you decide what might the best thing for you to choose out of your options? I suggest that you keep trying to expand the choices you see, and keep looking for new ones, especially when you think there are none!

Tough news? Maybe. But if you are willing to take the reins of your own life, there is no better news.

———◦———

CONCLUSIONS CONCERNING CHOICE

> It's (almost) all a choice!
> Life is filled with nothing but choices.
> Your life is composed of the consequences of your choices.
> Living itself is a choice.

The goal in life is to be able to see and make the existing choices which will promote health, happiness, and the positive outcomes you may desire. This may sound deceptively simple to you. But if you think it is easy, I have to say I admire your positive outlook! It takes persistence, but is SO worth it!

CHAPTER 6
THE GOOD FAIRY AIN'T COMING

THIS MAY WELL BE THE toughest Law of the Universe to accept, so I will get right to it:

> **> As much as we all wish it was not so, and as fervently we may pray for it to happen, my experience is that the Good Fairy simply ain't coming!**

Why on earth not? She may be too busy to help—or perhaps she does not truly exist. Whatever the case truly is, it does not pay to sit around waiting for her to come, sprinkle fairy dust over you, anoint you with her wand, and make you well. Believe me, I realize this is a bitter pill. We all want the Good Fairy to heal us. Wouldn't that be wonderfully easy, convenient, and effortless? It could even happen while we have dinner or watch a movie--and at the end of either, all our worries and concerns would be over!

Alas, the Good Fairy did not ever come to help me, and no magical changes or transformations took place in my life. I do hope she will come to your aid—but I am afraid you cannot count on her. You are likely to have the same experience I did.

I wish this were not so ... oh, how I have wished it would be easier for me and how I wish it could be easier for you! But I'm afraid it is best to prepare for the long haul—and the sooner you and I get used to this idea, the happier we will be and the more progress we will make in creating our own happiness and prosperity in the long run. It's simply not realistic to wait for improvement in our lives to magically occur!

I used to hope and wait, and even wish some other event (good or bad) might happen that would have the side effect of my anxiety disappearing. I actually entertained the possible advantages of having a small heart attack (if that very idea is not an oxymoron) because surviving it might impress on me how fortunate I was overall and help me get rid of what I considered to be my nagging, unnecessary, and unwarranted anxiety.

THE EARTH KEEPS SPINNING

It is a sobering realization that the world will keep spinning no matter how upset you may be, and that regardless of your negative feelings or outlook, the sun will continue to come up in the morning. But such is the case.

My observation of the world is that, unfortunately, it is filled with a tremendous amount of dysfunction, pain, and suffering. We may not share that suffering universally or to the same degree of intensity as another person we know, but it is amazing to learn over time the level of hurt, sorrow, guilt, regret, and subpar feelings and actions those among us may be suffering from. There is pain of all kinds in the world, and I feel deeply sorry for those who experience it.

But if you want a positive spin on the fact that the Good Fairy isn't coming, it would have to be that, if she were to come, she would rob you of the personal growth, satisfaction, and the increased empathy you achieve when you go through things on your own. When taking responsibility for what you think, do, and choose, you grow into a more complete and mature person. These are benefits that increase with the time and effort needed to achieve your goal!

So, don't be discouraged that the Good Fairy isn't materializing. You do not have to stay stuck, and you can really see progress if you work at improving yourself and taking advantage of your ability to find options and choose the ones which will benefit you and increase your personal and professional satisfaction in life. And yes, I know you may be saying, "I'll pass on the personal growth, thank you—just give me the cure and the change!" But life doesn't work that way.

As a matter of fact, at one point along my journey of writing this book, I used a working title of *Been There, Undone That.... Or What To Do Until the Good Fairy Arrives*. The best advice I can give is to read this book and follow the principles and strategies presented.

It is clear to me now that so much of our suffering and pain can be caused by our own deficiencies, our lack of knowing how to do things better or differently, our fear of change, and/or our negative mindsets. As frustrating as this news is, however, the good news is that the unwanted tendencies or lack of skills can be overcome and, to a significant extent, eliminated! This is a fact: I have done it myself, and so I know that you can as well.

As a further piece of good news, I'll discuss all of this in more detail and explain how to avail yourself of different ways to view and live your life in the chapters that follow.

CHAPTER 7
CHANGE HAPPENS!

ACCEPTING CHANGE

Possibly the only constant in the universe is change, and if you ever want to feel free, happy, and relaxed for very long, you had better get used to change. It is lovely to welcome change, but that is not what's essential. What is? To work towards being comfortable and confident that YOU CAN HANDLE IT. With that insight and progress, you are free; but without it, you are doomed to frustration and railing against the forces that be.

For many (most?) people, change causes anxiety at some level. However, I submit that this need not be the case. At a bare minimum you can improve your equanimity in the face of change by a combination of improvements in your:

> Acceptance of the way it is.
> Improving your self-image.
> Letting go of your ego.
> Persistence in trying to improve.
> Expanding your comfort zones.

Be willing to create change and temporary upsets; the world will not end because you do this!

> **Go for the best outcome even if it involves some upset, rather than settling for short-term peace by avoiding the effort to create a change.**

71

And since there is absolutely no way to avoid change in life, it is certainly more productive and stress-relieving to embrace change rather than fight it. As they say, it's easier to swim in the direction that the river is flowing. Trying to swim upstream (fighting change) is as difficult, tiring, and as stressful as anything you can do on an overall basis.

Sometimes people resist changing once something is set because they think it may reflect badly on them or would put them in an embarrassing situation. Those are not the important points to consider though! It's your life—you only get one as far as we know—and you are greatly advantaged by being comfortable with change.

When I've been faced with major changes in my life, after considering all options and effects as best I could, I have to say that I'm happy and satisfied with the decisions I made even though they may have put me in a potentially awkward or embarrassing situation in the short run. But it's the long run we should keep in mind!

Examples of significant changes I have had going down the road of life are as follows:

- Changed college majors, and therefore the rest of my life.
- Changed jobs once out of college, and that opened possibilities I couldn't have imagined previously.
- Permanently cancelled one medical operation, postponed a second one three days before it was to take place, and changed doctors and hospitals for a third operation. Each of these separate decisions turned out to be very much for the best.

TO GROW IS TO CHANGE

Someone has said that "to grow is to change." Certainly, you cannot grow without change because the terms are somewhat synonymous. Of course, you can change without positive growth, but let us hope that does not happen often!

At one time in my life, I spent decades trying to reach a state of peaceful stability with absolutely no more changes. But as Dr. Phil might ask, "How did that work for you?" I would have to admit, "Not well!" The more we want something, the harder it is to accept not getting it; and I suffered a great deal of frustration when I failed in reaching this impossible goal. I probably would have been much better off spending the time recognizing that my goal was unrealistic and impossible to achieve—and then getting on with things! This could have helped me avoid many of the unnecessary difficulties I visited upon myself.

We are not given to know the timing or nature of changes that will befall us, or even whether they will be good or bad. But it is certain that change will happen. The sooner you realize that change cannot be halted, and that the universe does not really care how fervently you hate change and want it to stop, the happier you will be. In fact, it may break you on the rocks of disappointment if you continue to resist! So, being comfortable with change is really for your own benefit. You stop swimming upstream and get at least a taste of "the peace that surpasses all understanding."

Listen to the universe.

Realize that you cannot control everything.

There will be many days when you realize there is relatively little you can actually control!

And that's okay.

———— ◉ ————

RESISTANCE AND PERSISTENCE

An important concept when dealing with changes in attitude is that resistance creates persistence. This is a concept I first heard almost a half century ago and it still rings true.

Resistance is like trying to swim upstream. It is exhausting and only serves to use up your resources and embed what you resist. Instead, if you can learn to accept what you cannot yet master while you are working towards the change you want, you will find it more relaxing and much like going with the flow.

Swimming upstream does nothing to diminish the power of the river. The river will continue (persist) forever, regardless of your efforts to resist.

Instead, if you focus on changing your mindset from resisting and efforting (swimming upstream) to acceptance, you can be in control.

When I used to have terrible bouts of conflict and panic attacks, I was never successful when all I did was try to fight them. They persisted no matter how much I resisted, insisted to myself that they had to go, or prayed they would disappear. It was only when I accepted that these feelings might always be with me to a degree and got off my rear end and used mitigating strategies, that my life changed.

Keep this thought in mind: The closest we can get to controlling what we cannot truly control is to accept it. This might take more than one reading to absorb, but it is worth your thought. In a very tangible way, this is like saying you snuggle with your demons.

Think of it this way: to stop a river, it takes a dam. This involves incredible forces and much work. On the other hand, all it takes to have a wonderful life of successfully navigating the same river is often just a small raft and a tiny rudder or paddle!

——————◦——————

ARE YOU RIDING A DEAD HORSE?

Regardless of the difficulty many of us have in making or dealing with changes, changes in life will continue. We know some changes can be stopped while others can only be slowed down; but in the big picture (our focus), they will happen! And in this context, we can think of our old ideas, positions, attitudes, etc. as "dead horses."

Discerning our dead horses isn't always easy. Sometimes it takes uncommon wisdom, and this rarely happens without an intentional process. Perhaps discernment begins with simply noticing, and not denying, a lack of forward movement. And then we discover that despite trying harder, being smarter, or being more aggressive, we stay at the same place! We may finally come to acknowledge that this same place is no longer our desired destination.

Some of us though must absolutely crash or tumble off the cliff before we really get the universe's message! But whatever it takes to get our attention, it is only by dismounting and letting go of our dead horse that we can begin a new journey.

This can be the very hardest thing we ever do! To best describe it, I'm going to use an amusing metaphor (giving credit to James R. Clapper and his extremely interesting book, *Facts & Fears*) and adding some other parts as well that I either created myself or found on the internet. The supposed tribal wisdom of the Dakota Indians, passed on from one generation to the next, explains what to do in a situation in which you find yourself riding a dead horse: When you discover you are riding a dead horse, the best strategy is dismount!

There may come a time in your life when something has run its course, or its time has passed; but for some reason it is difficult to let go. Anyone may think they are doing a great service by preserving the past, but this can be falling into the trap of "this is how it's always been done." That is easy. What isn't easy is looking at that horse and realizing his time is over, and then figuring out what the next step is.

You might be asking now why anyone (or any organization) would hold onto a dead horse. There are many reasons, among which are the following:

> We may have believed in the horse, hoped for the horse, and/or loved the horse.

> We doubted or denied the horse would ever die.

> Perhaps we relish the hero's role of resurrecting a dead horse, or the martyr's ideal of self-sacrifice alongside the horse.

> Dismounting seems to be giving up or doubting that there will ever be another live horse which we can ride again.

But start thinking about your life and ask yourself if you have ever done something analogous to an item on the list below. Some options may sound amusing, appealing, or enticing; but I don't recommend ANY of these strategies for getting that dead horse to move forward and win the race:

> Threatening the horse with termination.

> Appointing a committee to study the horse and/or revive him.

> Changing riders.

> Hiring outside contractors to ride the dead horse.

> Harnessing several dead horses together for increased speed or in the hopes one will spring to life and take off.

> Removing all obstacles in the dead horse's path.

> Providing additional training to any rider(s) of the dead horse.

> Declaring that riders who don't stay on dead horses are lazy, lack drive, and have no ambition—and then replacing them.

> Riding the dead horse smarter, not harder.

> Buying a stronger whip to get that dead horse moving.

> Providing added funding to increase the horse's performance.

> Doing a productivity study to see if lighter riders would improve the dead horse's performance.

> Purchasing an after-market product to make dead horses run faster, or acquiring an extended dead-horse warranty.

> Forming a quality focus group to find profitable uses for dead horses.

> Waiting for the horse's condition to improve from what you believe is a temporary downturn.

> Revising the performance requirements for all horses.

> Stating: A dead horse does not have to be fed, so it is more cost effective and requires less overhead and therefore contributes higher benefits to the mission than live horses.

> Arranging to visit other stables to see how they ride dead horses.

> Lowering the standards so that more dead horses can be included.

> Adopting a policy declaring this horse is not dead.

> Reclassifying the dead horse as "living impaired."

> Blaming the person who sold you the horse for it being dead when you bought it.

> Setting up a dead horse website or a GoFundMe account.

> Ignoring the condition of the dead horse and/or being in denial about it: "What dead horse? That horse is just fine! Look at that beautiful mane!"

> Naming the dead horse a "paradigm shift" and continuing to ride it.

> And if all else fails, promoting the dead horse to a supervisory position.

The take-away message is to be upfront, discerning, and realistic—and don't keep riding the dead horse!

CHAPTER 8

PERSEVERANCE BRINGS ABOUT THE DESIRED RESULTS

IN OUR LIVES, PERSEVERANCE is all important. As we have read, it is up to us to become aware of our available choices and create our own change—and since the Good Fairy ain't coming, it is up to us to make any desired change a reality.

How do we go about doing this?

› GET GOING AND KEEP WITH IT!

It is your whole life we are talking about here: The mental or emotional issue(s) you have or struggle with did not arrive overnight, and so they are unlikely to disappear overnight. The key is to keep working at them every day...24/7/365... to the maximum extent you can in order to have a happy, relaxed, productive future.

Some of you may think this sounds painful, hard, and burdensome. But realistically, what other choice is there? There simply is no other practical, productive option! Of course, you can curl up in a fetal position, get drunk, get high, and/or do other self-destructive things that reveal you don't know how to, or want to, develop good coping mechanisms. But that does not help you in any way; it simply prolongs your suffering and reduces your quality of life. Never doing the challenging work to improve may seem like an easy way to slide by; but this leads to discomfort or suffering for the rest of your life for, with, and from, your challenges, issues, and lack of skills. And as you age, the consequences from financial insecurity or the absence of nurturing relationships, etc. can become an increasingly heavy burden.

The other and better alternative is to keep working at it. In time you will be able to exert effort effortlessly, strive without stress, and achieve at an extremely high level almost reflexively. You will find yourself more relaxed and at peace, while performing far above average. You can be content in the knowledge that you have given your issues the appropriate attention and effort and that you are trying to take charge of your life and derive the most satisfaction possible.

———◦———

DON'T LET SETBACKS SET YOU BACK

Do not be discouraged when you have a setback, make a mistake, feel changes are not coming as they should, or have things going south. Such things will happen from time to time; and if you can acknowledge this from the start, you will be happier. It's just the way life works! STUFF HAPPENS! So, when it does, just get up and get back in the game without losing sight of what is at stake.

The Catholic religion has a number of strong examples of persistence but none more striking than in their Stations of the Cross prayers. In it, Jesus is forsaken and falls more than once, but He always gets up and goes on, sometimes alone and sometimes with help from another. Not only has He been deserted by His disciples, but He has suffered physical and psychological abuse and torture...and yet He GOES ON. Our problems may not be as serious as His were at the time of His Crucifixion, but we can apply His example to our own lives at times when we meet pain and suffering. As humans we will hit setbacks, and we will fail and fall from time to time; but what is important is to continue to get up again, and again, and again; and keep on striving to reach our goals.

Get back on the horse (of course, not that dead one!) each new day. Go from wherever you are, taking up the reins to your life and trying again! And then again and again.

Sometimes I feel I have saddle burns from having to get back on the horse so many times! But just because something may not be easy, why hesitate to try it again, especially if the payoff is a happier, more productive, and more content life with less stress, sadness, pain, and anxiety?

Isn't this what we all want?

Isn't this what you would want for yourself and your loved ones?

I can promise you that it is what your loved ones want for YOU!

It is better to continue to put forth the effort on important issues than it is to accept failure, sadness, disappointment, guilt, shame, regret, stress, anxiety, less-than desirable relationships, and/or the many other possible negative aspects of life. We will never reach anything close to our potential without perseverance. And the good news is that the kind of success we achieve after working hard like this is the sweetest and most meaningful reward that we can ever experience.

This may not be news, but it is true! Over time, you can see progress and change as you experience less suffering and more happiness and peace. The diligence is particularly important daily though, as is the need for trying to extend yourself and your abilities.

LONG-TERM EFFORTS FOR LONG-TERM RESULTS

The simple fact is that no one gets better at developing a meaningful skill without practice, patience, and hard work! Repetition helps things sink in and allows us to get it. With time and practice you can condition your body and mind to react as you like almost at once, simply by the fact that you have had repeated practice in what you are conditioning it to do. Think of basketball or baseball players—the number of reps they take is overwhelming to the rest of us, right? But not them!

I also have found that the more I use certain techniques (e.g. listening to music, meditating, or using a sleep apnea machine when I go to sleep), the more my body responds as if to say, "Okay ... so we are doing that now ... it's time to relax"—and now I relax almost immediately! In other words, my body has been trained to relax just from the THOUGHT of doing something, or from simply starting to do it, rather than having to go through the whole exercise to get any benefit from it.

This is an extension of the findings of Dr. Pavlov, in a way. The well-known psychologist found that by the repetition of ringing a bell before feeding dogs, the dogs would begin to salivate simply from the sound of the bell without him having to feed them. The silver lining here is: With practice and time, we can create a kind of Pavlovian response when it comes to relaxation or other skills we are striving to develop.

Thank you, Dr. Pavlov!

———◦———

WEEDING AND THE ONION

You may have heard that doing therapy is like peeling an onion, but what you may not have considered is the fact that in many cases that onion is an infinite one. You never really get there; but you can always feel even better, and find increased happiness.

A better analogy is to think of the process of becoming more mentally healthy as being similar to weeding a lawn or garden. To have a lawn (life) that is as lush and vibrant (happy and peaceful) as it can be, you will have to get rid of the trash and weeds (mental issues and unproductive ways of thinking or acting). As there can be any number of difficult species of weeds to deal with, you must be prepared with a whole variety of products and practices to get there. Often this will require extended effort over a period of time to get them down to the desired level.

To be able to effectively eliminate the weeds and improve your lawn, you have to get a good, firm, tight grip on where all the roots and tentacles originate and come together (the origins of the mental issues) before pulling hard on them to get them out of the ground. But even after having done this, you may find that part of the root system has broken off and remained despite your best efforts! You may have to dig deeper in the soil and work harder if you want to completely rid the lawn of these beasts.

Oh, and by the way...while you are weeding over there in the northwest corner of your garden, did you realize some other weeds are still growing in the southeast part...?

To sum it up: All too often taking care of your mental health and other issues just isn't easy, but keep PERSEVERING!

CHAPTER 9
THE PURSUIT OF EXCELLENCE TAKES PRIORITY OVER ATTEMPTS AT PERFECTION

"DON'T LET THE PERFECT be the enemy of the good."—Voltaire

I tend to be a very literal guy in many ways, so I take the goal of perfection as very serious and even dangerous. Instead, I am a strong proponent of the pursuit of excellence as opposed to perfection!

We will talk about accepting who we are in another chapter, but the reality is that some of us are compulsive perfectionists. As you know by now, I once was. I extend my sincere sympathies on a personal basis to those who still are. As Jim Taylor, Ph.D. Psychology said, "I have never met a happy perfectionist."

THE CASE FOR PERFECTION

Although in today's world, many view "obsessive compulsive" almost as four-letter words, it's important to acknowledge the huge positive aspect of the compulsive perfectionist's attitude. Remarkable things have been accomplished by perfectionists and those with a compulsive desire to succeed. The maniacal pursuit of a goal with little or no consideration of other factors and consequences, along with an indomitable will to succeed, has produced many of the great discoveries, advances, and accomplishments we revere and appreciate so much. This desire for perfection is easiest to see in top athletes, coaches, or the Steve Jobses or Nick Sabans of the world, who relentlessly drive themselves and those around them to achieve a goal. In his weekly articles in the *New Orleans Times-Picayune*, Mackie Shilstone, a fitness consultant to many high-profile professional athletes, often refers to their determination, preparation, commitment to excellence, unyielding drive to perfection, and perseverance.

And in terms of my own life, I can credit a good part of what I achieved in life to the drive and determination that came with my attempts to achieve perfection. But you have to consider the costs....

THE WHEELS ARE GOING TO FALL OFF THAT BUS ONE DAY

In my case, as a child I wanted more comfort, love, praise, and affection from my parents, and I tried to get this by being a perfect son. I tried to adhere to one of my dad's favorite sayings: "If it is worth doing, it's worth doing right!" Not giving my parents any reason to be disappointed in me resulted in success at home, as well as praise and status in school and sports, and later at work and in life in general. This positive reinforcement pretty much cemented my drive for perfection.

Everything worked out well for me until I could no longer juggle all the balls. After college, the wheels began to fall off the bus, and the balls I was juggling began to fall to the floor. The demands of a very difficult job, when added to my being only married for three or four years, expecting a second child with my wife, and studying for the CPA exam, caused weaknesses and cracks in my makeup. I previously had been able to hold everything together by sheer force of will; but I began to experience an elevated level of anxiety and panic attacks and began to lose control of my life.

It's true: The compulsive pursuit of perfection can screw up the rest of your life! It can kill you, drive you crazy, and/or create a stress level that is impossible to deal with successfully. Initially perfection may inspire you to do as much as you can to propel you toward enormous success—but this doesn't produce warmth, peace, relaxation, good relationships, or a generally happy life. I'm not alone in this experience and thinking. I have read a number of books, both those written from a psychological as well as biological point of view, which confirm this perspective.

QUALITY AND BALANCE COUNT

Like everything else in life, the emphasis you put on the quality of your effort is a choice you make as to the life you want to lead. You could say there is a continuum between lackadaisical living on the left, to balance and excellence towards the middle, and perfection on the right end. It is up to YOU—you, and no one else! —to decide where to set the button on the sliding control (think of the adjustments on a sound board with all those controls).

FYI, there isn't any preordained perfect setting here; indeed, it is simply a personal choice that is up to you; and you make the decision for yourself. You might do this consciously or unconsciously, but in either case it behooves you to know the tradeoffs! Also, you should understand that you are doing this with every action you take and each choice you make.

No two people will have the exact same definition of excellence vs. perfection even in a single endeavor; there are simply too many variables. And there is no formula or algorithm to employ. Instead, I suggest you check in with yourself to answer some general questions like:

> Are you happy and relaxed during the day?
> Do you sleep well at night?
> Are your goals set where you want them?
> Are you moving appropriately in the direction of achieving your goals?
> Will you feel satisfaction and completeness if you achieve your goals?

If you get any "no" answers to these, the corrections should be obvious (but not necessarily easy).

———◦———

TWEAKS VS. JERKS

Do you buy into the theory that there are two kinds of people: racehorses, and turtles? Well, if so, consider what might happen if that racehorse learns to relax at times? He will still be a racehorse, just one that is more calm, more productive, and likely to smell the roses from time to time. That racehorse may well win more races in the long run, now that he is a bit more chill! Granted, if you try to make a full-blown racehorse out of a turtle, you will kill it; and if you try to make a turtle out of a racehorse, the same outcome may occur. But we are not talking about such a drastic transformation. Just an adjustment. Try it!

ADJUSTING THE BUTTON

While I have been writing specifically about taking a step back from perfection, the very same things can be said about the excessive need to control or having other unhealthy compulsions. When you think about it, those terms are just forms of perfection from a layperson's point of view. This is a key point, but for the sake of brevity (of which I am rarely accused), I have lumped them together with perfection.

If you need things to be perfect, you are going to want to control them. Maybe you will think you have to do everything because no one else will do it right or do it your way. Delegation is not likely to be your strong suit. Also, you are going to want to control the environment to try to keep it all together. It seems to me that eventually this is going to negatively impact your inter-personal relationships and other important aspects of life, because:

> **When you try to control everything, you enjoy nothing!**

This last statement is very much akin to one of my favorite questions:

> **Do you want to be right, or do you want to be happy?**

To be honest, I do not think a day goes by when I don't remind myself of one or both of these valuable truths; and I think that any time you spend contemplating them is time very well spent!

So why not choose a new personal goal, setting aside the constant pursuit of perfection? That goal might be to

> Relax,

> Breathe deeply a little,

> Let go,

> Have confidence in your ability to handle whatever comes,

> Remember that very few of the things we worry about will happen or be important, and

> Just live...excellently!

Slide that adjustment button more towards "balanced." Stand down, relax, and go from perfection to excellence. A full-fledged perfectionist may resist this at first due to being uncomfortable with anything else as a goal as well as the worry that any slight relaxing will just be the first step on the slippery slope leading to degradation or being only average.

But not so. In my experience and opinion, there is little if any chance that a one-time perfectionist will become a slouch. It almost can't happen!

CHAPTER 10
THE PROBLEM IS NOT YOU

A GREAT DEAL OF SUFFERING in the world comes from people not accepting themselves. Because of all sorts of imaginary or unrealistic deficiencies on their part, they think they are unworthy of love or of having what they want. This pain could have arisen because someone once told them they are unworthy. Or perhaps they have done something they now regret or feel shame about, made a decision about themselves that is unwarranted, and/or they hurt others purposely or inadvertently. For all sorts of reasons these individuals now feel forever tainted by these comments, choices, or actions.

If you believe this about yourself, let me tell you something:

> Unless you persist in bad deeds on a continuing basis with malice of forethought, you are likely to be just fine!

> Despite most of the things for which you may fault yourself and regret, you are probably just fine! And,

> If you have unwanted and negative emotions and thought patterns, you may STILL be just fine!

In all likelihood, you are NORMAL! Your shortcomings in select areas are ones shared by many others. The only thing these supposedly terrible things show about you is that you are human. As members of humanity, we are ALL flawed!

In fact, there is a high probability that what you see as your horrible deficiencies are only unrealistic and critical judgements on your part. They may well be things you can go on to change or make up for, not universal truths or permanent conditions.

So lighten up and join the club—the club of being human, that is!

HAVING FLAWS IS PART OF BEING HUMAN

Think about this: Man is definitely a flawed species! We give in to unhealthy cravings like drugs, smoking and certain foods; indulge in excesses with alcohol and gambling; and suffer from mental illnesses, regrets, upsets, and all sorts of pain.

Even after thousands of years of civilization, humankind has not learned to live together in peace. Instead, we take our grievances to the point of starting wars. In today's world there are injustices, violence, hunger, poverty, and discrimination...we are certainly not as evolved as we could and might be! And this is just a sampling of things on a macro basis; the list of individual weaknesses, flaws, and vices is, unfortunately, quite lengthy.

Some of us act in cocky and arrogant ways, even if we don't feel confident on the inside. We might deliberately lie to friends and family, engage in a betrayal of our marriage by having an affair or by leaving our spouse, engage in temper tantrums or over-the-top displays of tears; or criticize and judge the others in our lives...even those we love the most, like our parents, children, and spouses.

ACCEPT AND FORGIVE YOURSELF AND OTHERS

Despite what I've just described as being characteristic of members of the human race, our goal as individuals is to learn to live with, embrace, accept, and love (yes, even <u>love</u>) the aspects of our personalities which, overall, deserve acceptance even if their existence indicates we are not perfect. We can and should love ourselves even if we don't have the nerve to speak up in public; have broken a promise to ourselves or another to do something; or nit-pick a colleague or family member when it is undeserved just because we ourselves are in a bad mood and choose to lash out at someone.

There's no benefit at all in being consumed by negative emotions and thoughts about ourselves! That alone does not move the needle in a positive-thinking or feeling direction.

As for those of us who believe they can hide the negative aspects of themselves from others—or even from themselves—the reality is we cannot! I believe our reactions to events and our interpersonal actions will always reflect our deep-seated feelings.

Instead of living in denial, forgive yourself and accept your weaknesses. Work on being truly free and at peace with yourself. It is well worth the effort!

IS IT A PROBLEM?

I was first introduced to the concept of having to accept rather than totally rid myself of what I considered my unwanted tendencies and flaws in my early 30's. There was a rather unusual set of circumstances going on in my life, and when I disclosed these to another person whom I was driving to the airport, he posed the following question to me:

> **WHAT IF YOU HAVE A PROBLEM, BUT HAVING A PROBLEM IS NOT A PROBLEM...DO YOU HAVE A PROBLEM?**

After thinking for a minute to try and understand exactly what he was asking and what I thought about it, I came back with this answer:

> **No ...THEN THE PROBLEM IS NOT REALLY A PROBLEM, IS IT?**

At that point, the person who had posed the question to me said my answer was correct—and that it might represent the best for which I could hope. His comment was a HUGE and mind-blowing awakening for me because, being a perfectionist, I had never even remotely considered any outcome other than total ANNIHILATION of my anxiety problem to be satisfactory!

After I dropped this man off and his response finally sank in, I pulled my car off the road and cried for a few minutes. While I felt some level of disappointment over the idea that I might never be able to meet my previous definition of being cured, I also experienced an indescribable release of energy and an increase in hope! There really WAS light at the end of the tunnel and a chance of getting to the point in my life where I could be at peace with myself without being perfect!

To say that this was a turning point in my life and one of the most impactful days I have ever had is a massive understatement. Without the possibility that I could come to accept and like myself even with what I had previously considered an unacceptable and major flaw, I'm not all sure I would be alive today...and I am positive I would never have had the same opportunities or successes I was able to achieve without this major, modifying experience. I don't think I could have withstood the stress and pressure for another 50+ years.

What I had experienced here was a version of, "when the student is ready, the teacher will appear." When I began that fateful day, I had only hoped to learn the secret to ridding myself of my issue, not that I could learn to accept it and live with it.

THE TIME AND EFFORT INVOLVED

No one ever said that self-acceptance is easy, however. Especially when you feel strongly about something, self-acceptance may require long-term and concentrated effort.

For example, when I retired I was looking forward to being able to fully relax. My objective was to stop having to push myself to try to improve. And although this may seem relatively mild or illogical to you, I was also hoping to be able to finally eat what I wanted without worrying about my weight.

As you might imagine, my objectives did not go smoothly or as planned. I found I would have to give up other important goals to follow these desires, and I did not like it one bit! For example, I realized clearly that being too overweight would negatively impact my health, happiness, and longevity, things that were quite serious and important to me.

But I also realized that, as is always the case, the universe did not care. It does what it does, and certain immutable laws are not subject to my wishes or intentions.

You too may be unlikely to totally rid yourself of what you are working on improving, since you and I, as members of the club of human beings, are likely to always have certain tendencies or behave in certain patterns. But please trust me and understand that this is really just fine and quite livable. You can like and approve of yourself overall when you accept that you can have problems that are not really problems!

NOT ALL GOOD, NOT ALL BAD

Here is a change in pattern you could embark upon for your self-improvement and self-acceptance journey: When you observe yourself going in a certain undesirable direction, you can then make whatever correction you think is appropriate and realistic. The correction can be quite small, and even if you don't fully realize your goal upon making the correction, you can be happy that you did this one thing. Good for you! You've made progress! Be grateful and proud of yourself for it.

Remember, there are few on off switches in life, few all good or all bad situations.

> **We live our lives on multidimensional continuums of interconnected sliding scales.**

We move left or right, up or down; and just as in geometry, we may live asymptotically (i.e. we may approach but never quite fully get to our goals). In my case, it was a goal of eliminating all bouts of anxiety from my life. But once we've made sufficient progress and learned to accept ourselves as we are, it no longer matters so much.

This, friends, is the sweet spot! Acceptance of ourselves is a choice we make along the path toward achieving peace. Please understand that I'm not talking about acceptance here as a way of avoiding making positive changes in any part of our work, home, or other aspects of our lives. I'm referring to a more general acceptance which comes after working hard to make the positive changes we can and want to make, and only then accepting the things we have not yet been able to change. Or perhaps we know we can and will do better with more practice, but we choose to be happy with our progress to date. The choices we make concerning our actions as well as our emotions, attitudes, and thoughts can bring peace beyond all measure. Eventually the body and spirit get very tired of swimming upstream. Self-acceptance can bring much-desired peace, rest, and calmness into our lives.

It may sound rather airy-fairy to tell you that acceptance, peace, and happiness are choices that we can make, as every single one of us can relate to certain areas or times when we fell short of those goals despite the best we had within us. But I maintain that the ability to make better choices for ourselves is real. What we need to do is improve our skills and get to the point where we are able to see and make the better choices. It can be done!

⸻ ◉ ⸻

GOING FORWARD

Concerning the things in life you may be called upon to experience, remember two important things:

1. You can accept what you cannot change or continue to struggle against it until hell freezes over. The universe doesn't really care what you do, and the world will keep turning either way. This leads to the second point....

2. Just as forgiveness is a gift you can give yourself, so too is acceptance. Acceptance is such an important gift to give to yourself, and it is your happiness that is enhanced when you accept. You are the primary beneficiary!

CHAPTER 11

"MISTAKES ARE THE PORTALS OF DISCOVERY"

- James Joyce (1882-1941)

LEARNING FROM MISTAKES AND LEARNING TO LIVE WITH THEM

Let's face it: We generally think of our mistakes as the bane of our existence. If there were no mistakes, we would all be still living in Eden, right? But we're not, and this means it behooves us to learn how to deal with mistakes so we can have the best possible life without letting them drain the vitality from our existence.

Life gives all of us hits and surprises, hurts and losses, and yes, dreaded, and uncomfortable mistakes—but it's how we deal with these and move on that determines our level of peace, equilibrium, and strength. Be aware...

> There is no such thing as arriving and never having to work on ourselves again. But...

> There is no end to the joy of forever growing.

So do not wish for no storms (or mistakes). Instead, learn to captain your vessel smoothly through the storms. It may take you a while to captain your vessel smoothly, but sail on and forward. As Mary Pickford, a great American actress, said:

> **"If you have made mistakes, even serious ones, there is always another chance for you. What we call failure is not the falling down but the staying down."**

TAKING IT HARD

As mentioned, for decades a simple mistake for me often triggered a long downward spiral of anxiety and resulting depression. This was followed by a bottoming-out at a pretty low level and then a long climb back to a relatively short-lived equilibrium.

My definition of a mistake was all-encompassing and usually involved me not being able to answer some obscure or meaningless question. I had set the bar for what constitutes a mistake at a rock-bottom level because I was that compulsive a perfectionist. I even used to think that if I worked hard enough, I might somehow eventually get to the time when I no longer had any mistakes or problems to deal with... WRONG! Not gonna' happen! In life there is a never-ending supply of challenges which lead to mistake possibilities, so mistakes continue to come no matter how low your mistake percentage gets.

As for readers who might harbor the thought in their mind that, "Okay, this guy says it is not realistic to avoid problems, and he could not do it—but (maybe) I can," let me give you a little mind-bender to consider:

> **The very fact that you even THINK you might get to the point of making no mistakes signifies you have actually made a HUGE mistake.**

How can this be? In order to think you have made no mistakes or won't make any in the future, you are one or more of the following:

> Likely to be delusional (never a good thing),

> Not pushing the limits sufficiently to reach your highest potential (not a good thing either), and/or

> Ignoring certain parts of life or endeavors which ultimately will limit you to a narrow field (perhaps you live, breathe, and die for

your career), and allow you to support the illusion of not making any mistakes in your life.

Each of these possibilities is a mistake ... BIG TIME! The immutable truth is that mistakes will always be with us. There are over 6 billion people on the planet and no two of us are exactly alike—but every one of us makes mistakes. You might think this is a bit of unwelcome news...but there is good news in play here that is more important:

> **Our mistakes do NOT define who we are unless we make them repeatedly and fail to learn from them. The key is to learn from them and move on.**

As the Dali Lama says: "Even if you lose the fight, do not lose the lesson." And as Dr. Paul Hokemeyer (mental health author and therapist) says: "It's OK to look back at the past, just don't stare."

With mistakes being inevitable, it certainly is in our best interest to learn to deal productively and responsibly with them!

LAUGH ABOUT THEM

Wouldn't it be wonderful to learn to accept our errors and perhaps even enjoy them....to be able to use them as a "feel-good laugh" at ourselves and as a learning experience? With practice this is indeed possible. It's something I've done myself.

Making mistakes, no matter their size, used to affect me so intensely that I had to learn to keep breathing, figuratively and literally! For me, the resulting shock and feeling of disaster tended to make me hold my breath, begin to sweat, and cause my anxiety level shoot up. Eventually I discovered that the more I breathed normally, the easier it was to get beyond the mistake. And then I discovered that laughing at the situation (or at myself for making the mistake) proved the best reaction of all, whenever it was appropriate to do so. There's a practical reason it worked so well for me: Laughing involves expelling air followed by normal breathing, and so it never failed to make me feel better physically. It also helped me simply to relax and regain my perspective. Besides, the laughter sends a subtle message to others that this is such a small, trivial event, and so unlike me to do, that it's funny. Also, it buys a few seconds of calm and changes the flow of the conversation.

If I could learn to laugh at my mistakes, so can you! This is a great reaction if your mistake is a more normal or commonplace one, versus an industrial-sized mistake which might involve a great deal of shame and regret. You want to be able to laugh about the normal ones, and as I said above, learn from them and move on. Of course, this may be easy to write, but not always easy to do. Far too many of us feel that mistakes make us wrong or bad, and because we find the thought of being wrong so disagreeable, we try to justify or deny our mistakes and/or try to make them disappear. Well, this keeps us stuck and deprives us of freedom and spontaneity in our lives. By not acknowledging our errors and instead fighting against the idea that we've made a mistake, we remain stuck. Remember the statement above – what we resist, persists!

> **Our mistakes are an opportunity for a breakthrough, a chance to learn and laugh, a way to grow and improve our lives and relationships, and a way to move forward!!!**

The goal here is to move as close as you can to accepting and embracing this concept!

------•------

GET COMFORTABLE

If you find yourself having difficulty acknowledging your mistakes, consider an experiment in which you purposely screw up but choose to do so freely and without concern or self-judgment. Then, just like a research scientist would, observe (as objectively as possible) the effect doing this has on you and others around you.

You will probably find that you feel much better, more open, and honest. At first this may feel odd, but the difficulty should melt away in a relatively brief time when you look at how you feel and also how others react. When you freely acknowledge your errors, the reaction you get from others involved is likely to be one of forgiveness and understanding. When you argue about or try to deny your mistakes, it doesn't sit well with others; and they are more likely to argue with or blame you. People who are open and honest about what they have done in error hold an incredible appeal for many folks. This may come as a shocking surprise to some; but when you encounter people who are open, it forges a strong connection and bond of trust that serves as a huge plus to all parties. Consider this:

> **It's not what happens in your life that counts, even the making of mistakes. What matters is how you deal with the situation(s) and what you do next.**

Those comfortable with themselves are not defensive when it comes to making mistakes and have nothing to prove. For example, now that I am more comfortable in my own skin and no longer feel that my mistakes or errors define me, I always try to be the first to acknowledge my shortcomings. Generally, I find laughing at my mistakes to be the most effective and enjoyable way of dealing with them, and I do my best to never to deny or argue about them. Acting this way tends to minimize the significance of most errors, puts others at ease, and reduces any tension that may otherwise exist. Now I laugh at myself, the mistake, and the very thought that anyone would place any real importance on a simple mistake. And others usually laugh too when I do. I then apologize if it's appropriate and move on. Naturally of course, I also correct the mistake and/or tell the other party that I do not intend to make that mistake again.

I've even come to believe our reaction to our mistakes can be used as a great test of our mental health! I consider each of the following to be a sign of good mental health:

> Being willing to make mistakes.

> Choosing to reach out and try new things, even if we are not good or experienced at them.

> Stepping out of our comfort zone, and thereby risking screwups.

> Getting comfortable with the phrases, "I'm wrong" or "I don't know." For some of us these words do not come easily, and while this may have something to do with the reaction we receive from others when we acknowledge our errors, it is likely to be more what is going on in our own heads. Still, it is good to make these acknowledgements.

⊙

LEARN AND ADJUST

Mistakes are like the gutters of life, and we often learn by lurching from one mistake to another. Just as it can happen with driving, going from a gutter on one side of the road to the one on the other side, trying not to overcorrect, we always try to return to equilibrium before any real damage is done. Most of our learning comes from trying to keep things going down some version of the middle of the road, but if you fail to adjust as necessary and run into a ditch before correcting again, there still is much you can learn from that experience. So focus on that! Perhaps this is not the highest and best manner of learning, but it can be effective nonetheless and certainly is common. It is always best to use our higher selves and our thinking skills to learn in other, less painful ways; but the only real tragedy of this situation is not learning and growing after we make a mistake.

Coming to accept my mistakes did not occur overnight for me; but it did take place! It took me a long time (30 years+/-), and I have immense satisfaction looking back at my progress, for life has been far richer and enjoyable as a result. Hopefully, you can achieve this much faster than I did; but it is, at the end of the day, simply a matter of broadening your perspective, training yourself, and exercising some control over your mind. It is worth the effort and the practice!

CHAPTER 12

DELAYED GRATIFICATION IS ESSENTIAL TO LIVING OUR BEST LIVES

IT'S TRUE THAT WE ALL crave immediate gratification—getting something we want right away—but our need to appreciate and practice delayed gratification is essential to living our happiest and most productive lives. Why? Because it sure beats the hell out of immediately capitulating to what might be only a shiny object, a quick fix, or a short-term solution that leaves us wanting in the long run!

> **Unless we learn how to avoid letting our emotions and desires of the moment control us, there is no way to have our most peaceful and satisfying lives.**

To ultimately be happy, we need to be in control of our emotions and urges. This is definitely a skill that needs to be learned and honed! We should control our urges, not vice versa! The more we are, and the more we feel in control, the happier and more relaxed we will be.

Early in my own life, I was very willing to adopt the principle of delayed gratification to succeed at what I desired most: to reduce my anxiety and panic attacks. And once I started getting there, I experienced a thrill of that victory that was almost impossible to describe!

We need to stretch or expand the control we have over our minds and our emotions—to a minute, an hour, a day, a week at a time. It really is a simple system, conceptually, although I must acknowledge that my family sometimes still tells me I need to continue my work on this skill, especially when it comes to productivity-enhancing electronics.

On the other hand, I have chosen not to smoke, drink alcohol, take non-prescription drugs, gamble, or engage in an exceptionally large number of other common diversionary activities. I also have worked to master delayed gratification in the big areas of succeeding at work and sacrificing for 70+ years to achieve the major personal goals I set for myself: attaining and enjoying peace, reducing my anxiety, and thinking positively most often to achieve more happiness in my life.

———◦———

HOW DO WE MASTER THIS LOU?

This chapter is going to be short, simply because there are no hard and fast rules or guidelines as to how to master the skill of delayed gratification. Each of us is a mass of contradictions, conundrums, mysteries, talents, tendencies, deficiencies, and different character traits. This results in some of us doing well in some aspects of our lives and not so well in others. And other members in our club of humans may hold traits and tendencies which are exactly the opposite of ours!

So some of us may be able to lose weight but can't put down the cigarette; others might be able to move out of depression by working on their coping skills over time but be unable to overcome an incident from childhood; and still others might be able to stop smoking, but not find peace or happiness in their daily lives.

My suggestion for you is simply...

> **Begin, and never stop until you reach your goal(s), particularly those that you know are best for you in the long run!**

Ultimately, it is up to each of us to proceed on our individual path and at our own pace. We work on acquiring different skills and moving towards long-term goals, finding and developing our own balance with whatever combination of factors and personality facets that entails, so that we are content during the day and at peace with ourselves when our heads hit the pillow at night.

Simply be willing to sacrifice in the short term for a worthy long term goal.

CHAPTER 13
HAVE AND EXPAND PERSPECTIVE

THE ABILITY TO HAVE perspective on what is concerning us or others is one the most important mental attributes we can improve. It's also important to explain why I personally assign it such a high priority.

When I was in my early twenties, my compulsive, perfectionistic personality made it almost impossible to have any sort of perspective on things; and the lack of this happened to be one of the first deficiencies I recognized in myself. Without perspective and while pursuing perfection in everything, I had no gratitude, no peace, no relaxation, no rest, and no calm focus on one thing at a time! It is precisely these deficiencies and others which can be cured by perspective.

Without perspective, I jumped from crisis to crisis putting out fires and trying to keep everything under control. Without perspective, my life was a living hell! Just think of it ... how can a person ever experience peace and love if every little thing is disruptive to their perfect ideal? And when it came to that perfectionist youthful me, any ripple that upset my apple cart was a BIG, BIG deal!

The fact is that perspective and perfection cannot coexist. Perspective is the antithesis of striving for perfection. Instead of encouraging the open, broader view that having perspective allows us, perfection feeds into compulsiveness, which diminishes perspective.

Back in my 20's I had as close to a "no shell, no perspective," life as a person can have. I had no overall source of calm or any idea of my self-worth. Individual victories and successes were not lasting, and true peace was nowhere to be found. The "atta boy, awww s@#*!" system I've mentioned prevented me from experiencing any sort of peace. Nonetheless, I remained totally committed to keeping my perfectionistic outlook while trying to develop a shell at the same time...until, FINALLY, I came to realize I could not succeed if I continued to do this. I doubt that anyone can. I saw that trying to achieve perfection was impossible, and not even desirable. Perfection was neither achievable nor even a worthy goal. It was not good, and it was not realistic. It was not a worthwhile goal or attitude—and ever since then I have been working to improve and expand my perspective.

HOW PERSPECTIVE HELPS

Let me give you an analogy of why perspective is so important. I have a bad shoulder which has no remaining cartilage; it is bone on bone with resulting discomfort at times and reduced mobility. I equate this physical issue to the mental aspects of perfection and perspective. Perspective functions like cartilage – it softens blows, increases mobility in thoughts and actions, and cushions against pain. And in this analogy, perfection is the equivalent of having no cartilage. It narrows the field of comfort, increases the pain of stress and anxiety, and generally creates a more jolting and a painful life.

Today I am generally able to weather life's upsets involving my relationships, family, career, and so on, with calmness and equanimity. That's quite different from how I reacted in the old days of my youth, and I am incredibly grateful for what I have attained.

WHAT'S GOING ON IN YOUR HEAD?

But now let's talk about you...You've picked up this book in an effort to change and improve your life, so let's look at how you might feel about your life right now:

> Do you perhaps think that what's going on in your life is simply the worst set of circumstances in the world, and that no one else can possibly be as miserable as you are?

> Do you believe that no one understands how hard you try or what you're going through?

> Do you think there's no way out? That you are stuck, and have no options?

> Do you think that others, whose beliefs are different from yours, are wrong? And perhaps that they're even fools for the beliefs they hold (religious, political, cultural, etc.) and for how they are choosing to live their lives?

If you nodded your head "yes" after any of these questions, perhaps you could use a bit more perspective. It is worthwhile work indeed, and you can improve your perspective and empathy.

So just how might you go about that?

---

17 WAYS TO GAIN PERSPECTIVE

Below are over 17 ways that have helped me over 60 years of working on this issue. Choose the way or ways that appeal to you and trigger your own creativity in this area. Okay, let's go!

1. If you feel you have problems, stand up (or stay seated and hold up your arm if that works better for you). The following is a list of increasingly serious issues that everyday people just like us might experience. As you read this list, continue to stand, or hold your arm up for as long as you think your issues are at least as serious as the ones on the list. Once your issues no longer seem as serious as the ones on the list, you may lower your arm or be seated. In other words, you are to sit down when you would no longer trade places with someone who had the issues you have read on the list. Nonetheless, I want you to read the entire list; don't stop reading once you stand down!

That's because I have a few questions I want you to respond to after you get through the list.

Ready? Here goes!

<u>HOW BAD ARE YOUR PROBLEMS ... REALLY?</u>

> You have a hangnail, literally.

> You are juggling responsibilities—children, home, career, and so on.

> You are frustrated by people not doing their jobs properly, such as when you are dealing with customer service or other poorly trained service personnel.

> You have to correct errors made by others.

> You have time pressures with too much to do in the time period available to you.

> Everything costs too much.

> You feel that you continually make bad choices.

> You do not have the time for family or friends, or for those activities in which you would like to be involved.

> You or a member of your family feels pressured financially, socially, or ethically.

> You are a professional coach and your entire season as well as your career just got blown apart because someone failed to properly count to three, catch a ball that hit them in the hands, or perform some other activity that they had practiced at least 1,000 times. Or perhaps you are a farmer and a full year's harvest is wiped away by too much or too little rain, a freeze, too much heat, or some small insect. Or...

> You lose your job.

> You feel you have insufficient education and see no economic future for yourself.

> You are unable to read.

> You have no home or are going to lose your home or lease.

> You have an ongoing problem of not having enough money and so you cannot eat properly; thus, you are constantly hungry and in poor health.

> You do not have enough money for anything beyond the basic necessities of life.

> You are the caregiver for an aging family member who is in a deteriorating condition.

> A meaningful relationship has turned sour and has been terminated.

> You have lost a loved one or friend.

> You do not have enough money even for basic necessities and difficult choices are needed.

> Someone you love is in jail in the US.

> You do not have access to clean drinking water.

> You are in a situation where animals are being abused.

> You or a loved one has been mugged and is psychologically shaken.

> You, your significant other, or your children are being cruelly abused (or have been abused) physically, sexually, and/or

mentally, and all involved parties are dealing with the issues related to that. (The abuse could have been caused by a parent, family member, stranger, etc.)

> A loved one is in jail in a foreign country, and you are in fear of the conditions which they will have to endure while in that jail.

> You or a loved one is addicted to a harmful substance.

> Your parents are drug addicts.

> You have lost one or more limbs or are physically crippled.

> Your brain does not respond normally, and you have lost one or more of your senses (e.g. you are blind, or deaf).

> You or a loved one are beset with a mental disorder that leaves you in constant fear, worry, anxiety, guilt, shame, regret and/or other condition.

> You or a loved one is severely hurt in an accident.

> You, your significant other, or your children are in serious, constant, debilitating pain.

> You or a loved one has been diagnosed with a terminal disease.

> You or a loved one has been diagnosed with a terminal disease and there is no effective way to ease the pain.

> You or someone you care about is being tortured.

> You have lost a child to illness.

> You have lost a child or other loved one to suicide.

> You have lost a loved one or friend to gang violence, police brutality, or as a result of discrimination.

> You have witnessed a friend or loved one killed suddenly right next to you.

> You have lost a child or loved one due to a drunk driver.

> Large numbers of people are being killed by diseases, epidemics, or wars which seem to have no end.

Unfortunately, this is far from a complete listing of the ills experienced by people every day in our world. And given a certain set of circumstances, they could be happening to any of us.

So, having read this list, how do you now feel about your current problems? Has the exercise been helpful in giving you perspective and gratitude for what you have in your life compared to what others are experiencing in their lives? (I do pray that your arm is not still up in the air or that you are not still standing, and that you have long since realized your correct place on the continuum.)

The reality is, almost all of us have a tremendous amount to be grateful for in our daily lives, and it is certainly valid to be grateful for not being worse off than you are.

Perspective can offer this feeling of gratitude to you, and ease what would otherwise be a consuming "woe is me!" attitude.

2. I have met only a very few people in my life who, from time to time, did not feel sorry for themselves. At this moment, I want you to think about whether you currently are starring as the main character of "The Cross Room" below. (Interestingly, the same story exists in both the Christian as well as the Jewish tradition.)

The Cross Room

The young man was at the end of his rope.
Seeing no way out, he dropped to his knees in prayer.
"Lord, I can't go on," he said.
"I have too heavy a cross to bear."
The Lord replied,
"My son, if you can't bear its weight,
just place your cross inside this room.

Then open another door and pick any cross you wish."
The man was filled with relief.
"Thank you, Lord," he sighed, and did as he was told.
As he looked around the room he saw many different crosses;
some so large the tops were not visible.
Then he spotted a tiny cross leaning against a far wall.
"I'd like that one, Lord,"
he whispered. And the Lord replied,
"My son, that's the cross you brought in."
Written by
Unknown

Pressures from various parts of life can build up until there seems to be no light at the end of the tunnel, and we see no way to cope with or manage what has to be done. Yet things are rarely as bad as we think when we are in such a situation, and remembering this can be extremely helpful. Too many of us perceive (probably incorrectly) there are others who seem never to have such issues. All of us might find remembering the message of "The Cross Room" to be a tremendous help in terms of gaining perspective.

As an incredibly wise soul once told me, when we are wearing fecal-colored glasses, the world tends to look a little s#%&&y!

3. Choose to develop and engage your perspective. As with so many other things in life, perspective is a choice; and it is extremely far-reaching, just like adopting a positive mental attitude proves to be. Just remember that you CAN change and improve. There simply is no question about this.

But it is up to you. So, work on gaining perspective! Try hard, and never give up: The outcome is only a function of your motivation and determination.

Those of you who lack perspective might tell yourself, "This is just the way I am," or "I can't change." That just isn't so! However, you must continue to work hard to get the absolute best results.

It is almost funny to think that there are "naturals" out there who just do the right thing, have the right attitude, and always perform flawlessly with no effort. I suppose there may actually be a few of those (one of them being Barbara Streisand), but it's a darned few!

Virtually all the people we see and know of who have achieved goals and accomplished remarkable things have worked their rear ends off to do this! If you choose to read the biographies or autobiographies of many world leaders, skilled athletes, scientists, statesmen, military leaders, famous entertainers, and so forth, you will discover the circumstances from which they came, the challenges with which they had to deal, and how hard they had to work for their success. Often it takes decades of work to be an overnight sensation or to make things look easy.

You must be committed to your purpose, and unrelenting in pursuit of your goal of gaining perspective because it isn't always easy. Live and breathe it; be passionate and unyielding in your efforts.

4. Look OUTWARD rather than INWARD.

When I was anxious and it crippled my life, I tended to have tunnel vision. At times like this, I was fixated primarily on myself...so much so that I temporarily lost my peripheral vision as well as any sense of humor! Not only was I unable to make a joke, but if someone tried to tell a joke, I usually looked at them like they had three heads and wondered why the hell they had just said what they did. I was totally in survival mode, so I found nothing funny.

If our focus is on ourselves, it is easier to catastrophize, making even a hangnail seems like a real issue. Yet a hangnail would not be in the consciousness of a Navy Seal during a mission or a surgeon who is performing an operation. The wider our perspective and the more we focus OUTWARD, the less trivial matters will be a concern of ours.

So, look at what bothers you ...could you benefit from a broader perspective? It is extremely helpful both to force yourself to look outward rather than inward, and to interact with others.

5. Do not exaggerate your own weaknesses; instead, assess your weaknesses realistically. Many people fault themselves and lead limited lives because they see themselves as weak, stupid, mean-spirited, etc. due to what are, in actuality, inappropriate decisions or actions taken long ago by themselves and/or others...so long ago that no one other than themselves really remembers or cares about them!

We can be the source of our own guilt and a lack of self-confidence for having made incorrect or illogical decisions, or coming to flawed conclusions when we are young. Guilt and judgment are self-imposed and limit us. Sadly, we can go on for decades—even a lifetime—without ever challenging or correcting such beliefs or assumptions. Seeing others and realizing how they (all of us) have weaknesses and make mistakes can lessen the sting of our own issues or errors.

Perspective helps us realize what is normal and natural. Move past blaming and being ashamed of yourself!

6. Remember the French saying, "What makes us discontented with our condition is the absurdly exaggerated idea we have of the happiness (or lack of problems) of others." (Note: I added the previous parenthetical.) Realizing the truth of this helps with, and is part of, having perspective. Another point to remember is that, if you compare yourself to others, you are comparing their outside to your inside! Obviously, this is not an apples-to-apples comparison. Almost everyone can look one way on the outside but feel and be completely different on the inside.

As author Geneen Roth points out:

> No one has a life in which only the good stuff is there while all the pain is gone. Harmful stuff and pain happen. We all have pain, torments, wounds, hurts, and/or abandonment.... The quality of life has much to do with how well we deal with the pain.

> The purpose of healing is not to be forever happy— that is not possible. The purpose of healing is to be awake and live while you're alive. There is no such thing as arriving and never having to work on yourself again. You don't get past emotional issues. There are few things in my life that I get past. I just get comfortable with them....

I would only add to this the reminder for us all that, while time heals all wounds, it also wounds all heels. Wounds shape the curves of our lives like a river shapes its banks. We are both scarred and polished by time.

Also, wounds can build up on the banks of the river of our lives just as plaque in our arteries; and if allowed to accumulate over time, a mind attack, perhaps in the form of anxiety, can occur just as a heart attack can happen in the circulatory system.

7. An epiphany can open up your life. An epiphany is defined as "a sudden, intuitive perception of, or insight into the reality or essential meaning of something, usually initiated by some simple, or commonplace occurrence or experience." It feels like having all of the tumblers of the universe simultaneously line up, so you feel that you see things with enhanced clarity, or you feel you are being tapped on the shoulder and given a message directly from your Higher Power.

If you are fortunate enough to experience such an "ah-ha" moment in your life, I strongly recommend that you keep any good feelings associated with the epiphany ever-present in your mind. Such experiences are like messages from the universe directly to you and can create vast improvements in your perspective.

I realize that many may say they have never had an epiphany; but I have been fortunate enough to have had a number of them, and I am incredibly grateful for each. They occurred in almost each decade of my life since my teens, and each time I was left with an indescribable feeling of peace and clarity. Some of my most valuable epiphanies were:

> I had to accept my issues and stop all of my flailing around to completely rid myself of them. "If you had a problem, but having the problem was not really a problem, then did I really have a problem?"

> Anxiety can't coexist with gratitude, or the feeling generated by helping others.

> Realizing, at a particular time, that my primary job as a parent was over, and that I could concentrate more on being great friends with my children.

8. Choose the right song to change or manage your mood.

Songs can help us gain perspective. Many tell a story that provides some lesson or conveys some feeling that improves our perspective. Here are some of my favorites; but of course, you should come up with your own preferences:

> "What Doesn't Kill You Makes You Stronger" by Julie Strong

> "Blind Man in the Bleachers" by Kenny Star

> "Here Comes That Rainbow Again" by Kris Kristofferson

> "The Greatest" by Kenny Rogers

> "I Will Survive" by Gloria Gaynor. (By the way, aside from this song, Gloria Gaynor co-authored a book with Sue Carswell, *We Will Survive,* about the incredible stories of some people who faced horrible situations and not only survived but went on to thrive. It is a very inspirational book and puts the mundane issues that most of us have very much in perspective. Upon reading it, you may discover it is almost unavoidable to consider your own situation and feel better! Compared to what some people have to face, your issues, even when painful or sad in and of themselves, are not as bad as you think they are if you take on a bigger perspective. If other folks can overcome their huge incidents, there is hope for the rest of us.)

9. Consider the following information – which may no longer be completely up to date, but does provide a glimpse of how many of the people in the world live on a daily basis – then, stop and think about your own life.
Perspectives On Our World:

> If your parents are still alive and still married, you are a rare individual.

> If someone sent you this message, you're extremely lucky because someone is thinking of you and also because you don't comprise one of the 2 billion people unable to read.

> If you currently have money in the bank and your wallet, you are among the privileged few – only 8% of the world's population is in this group.

> If you can go to your place of worship without fear that someone will assault or kill you, then you are luckier than 3 billion people.

> If you have a full fridge, clothes on your back, a roof over your head and a place to sleep, you are wealthier than 75% of the world's population.

> If you have never experienced the horror of war, the solitude of prison, and/or the pain of torture, and have never been close to death from starvation, then you are better off than 500 million people.

> If you woke up this morning in good health, you would have more luck than the one million people who won't live through the week.

> If you could fit the entire population of the world into a village consisting of 100 people, while maintaining the proportions of all the people living on Earth, that village would consist of:

- 57 Asians
- 21 Europeans
- 14 Americans (North, Central and South)
- 8 Africans

> But consider again the following:

- 6 people would possess 59% of the wealth and all would come from the USA
- 80 would live in poverty
- 70 would be illiterate
- 50 would suffer from hunger and malnutrition

- 1 would be dying
- 1 would be being born
- 1 would own a computer
- 1 (yes, only one) would have a university degree
- There would be:
    ◦ 52 women and 48 men
    ◦ 30 Caucasians and 70 non-Caucasians
    ◦ 30 Christians and 70 non-Christians
    ◦ 89 heterosexuals and 11 non-heterosexual people

If we looked at the world in this way, the need for acceptance and understanding is obvious. We ARE all cut from the same loaf—just toasted a little differently!

Takeaways:

> **Work** like you don't need the money.
> **Love** like nobody ever hurt you.
> **Dance** like nobody is watching.
> **Sing** like nobody is listening.
> **Live** as if this were paradise on Earth.

-Old and anonymous internet posting

10. Reflect on "The Pale Blue Dot."

I first read astronomer Carl Sagan's article, "The Pale Blue Dot" in the September 9, 1990, issue of *Parade* magazine. It was accompanied by a Voyager 1 picture looking back at the earth from 3.6 billion miles away in space. Sagan's message is extremely helpful to us in keeping our perspective. This picture makes our earth look like a tiny blue speck floating in a sea of blackness. Yet, as he points out, it has been the only home of the known intelligent beings. This is where humankind has experienced all emotions, conceived all known thought, and the only place in the seemingly endless universe that man has lived, efforted, accomplished remarkable things, failed, advanced science and the arts, and, on an individual basis, has ultimately died. Everything that has happened to humankind, every emotion ever felt, every belief ever held, and every war ever waged has taken place on this tiny "mote of dust suspended in a sunbeam."

Our self-importance and hubris is challenged by this view of our entire planet as nothing more than a "lonely speck in the vast and enveloping cosmic dark." Sagan notes that even our sun is nothing more than a "humdrum star in the outskirts of a galaxy of hundreds of billions of such stars", and that "even our galaxy is only one of uncounted billions of galaxies in the universe."

Does this have an impact on how you feel and how you view your individual issues? It does for me! The resulting change in perspective allows me to be more aware of how we fit in and the importance (or not) of what I was dealing with at the time.

11. To increase your perspective, think about how the time that man has been on the planet compares to the total time since the "Big Bang "and the time that earth has been in existence.

In the article, "The Truth is Out There," Lynn Sherry, a noted scientist, offers a cosmic calendar that compresses 13.8 billion years (the time since the Big Bang) into a single year-at-a-glance in which humans arrive only in the last few seconds of that year. I find this calendar immensely helpful at times to realize how very recently humans and even the earth have been in existence, and how insignificant and petty most of my concerns are when compared to the universe and all that has gone on since the Big Bang.

12. Next I would like you to avail yourself of information on the sizes of various objects (both very large and very small) which surround us at all times. This knowledge should prove humbling! You can easily find an award-winning presentation of this, which I heartily recommend by entering "Cosmic Eye – Louise 2012" in Google. There are several versions of the same video, but I consider the longer ones (3:01 and 3:32 minutes) to be the best.

13. "The crisis of today is the joke of tomorrow."
- H. G. Wells, English author (1866-1946)

This quote offers a valuable reminder to relax or take a step back in terms of what pains or concerns us at the moment.

It is always difficult (indeed, impossible) to see ahead with any certainty and know the actual outcome of a current situation that distresses you. It is much easier to take a few deep breaths, chill out, and think back to how many past crises-of-the-moment turned out to be nothing more than a blip in your life —and may have even become something about which you can now chuckle on your own or with others.

Our very DNA literally programs our minds to go into "Danger! Danger, Will Robinson" mode when there's a crisis —but how many of our so-called snafus of the past have really made an enduring impact on us and our lives? Are any even meaningful today? Most fizzle out and don't ultimately have even a fraction of the impact we are fearful of at first. If you are able to keep this in mind, it can make a significant difference.

My parents used to tell me, "Twenty years from now this will not matter." The sooner you internalize this wonderful advice, the sooner and more easily you will get over life's inevitable bumps in the road.

14. "Life is 10% what you make it, and 90% how you take it."

- Irving Berlin, American songwriter (1888–1989)

What Irving Berlin said is true! Happiness is not about getting more of anything, or everything. It's the ability to:

> Deal effectively with what's currently happening and the attitude you are bringing to it;

> See what's happening and be appropriately interested or engaged in it; and

> Want what you have (not necessarily have what you want).

Friends, THIS IS *IT!* This is your life ... now! Your very happiness depends on how you deal with the stuff life presents. Replace what you think of as problems with a mixture of action, acceptance, understanding, and self-love. To thrive in life, all of us need the following:

> A good self-image;
> A protective but empathetic shell;
> Perspective;
> Gratitude.

15. Keep in mind the 18/40/60 principle. It says:

> At 18 you worry about what people may be saying about you.
> At 40 you know pretty well what people are saying about you.
> At 60 you don't care what people are saying about you.

The sooner you can get to the mindset in step C, the better! (My heartfelt thanks to psychiatrist Daniel Amen for including this rule in his book, *Change Your Brain, Change Your Life.*)

Yes, a little age definitely helps you realize what is and what isn't important.

16. Understand that POTUS is probably sleeping better than you.

Another lesson I had on perspective came from a parking attendant I knew. He frequently talked to himself aloud, and it seemed whenever I drove my car into his lot and overheard him, he was having a horrible day. He complained about the weather, his customers and their demands, his bosses and their requirements, and how he needed help to run the lot. This went on day in, day out, day after day. Needless to say, this is NOT an uplifting way to begin a day or live the day! This man seemed to honestly feel he was the most put-upon and troubled soul in the city. Yet how could that be when I had reserved that very title for myself?

I learned an important lesson from his attitude, and what his problems had to say about the very things that troubled me so much. I realized that just as I thought this troubled parking attendant's problems were far less severe than he did, many people would look at what *I* thought were very troubling issues and not find them troubling at all. I could only laugh as I took it a step further and reached the realization that POTUS, who truly has the weight of the world on his shoulders, was probably sleeping better than I was....so clearly there had to be something wrong with my way of thinking!

What an enormously powerful lesson for me about perspective. I hope it will be meaningful to you as well.

17. Here are suggestions for what to do if you are a fellow sufferer in the perfection or compulsion traps, or if you simply want to expand your perspective:

> Remember that perfection and compulsions cannot coexist with perspective, and the more you have of the latter, the less you will suffer from the former.

> Work like hell to change by harnessing your drive and determination to beat any addiction to perfection and to expand your perspective.

> Let it be . . . and learn to let things go!

> Think, "Who really cares? What difference does it really make? Will it matter ten months from now? Twenty years from now?"

> Learn to laugh at yourself and your mistakes as well as your knee-jerk negative feelings about them. This is incredibly powerful, and it is now my first reaction to a screwup (so yes, I laugh a lot!).

> Set realistic, achievable goals.

> Don't task yourself with being the best in every situation; just start off with a reasonable and achievable goal and then build on that.

> Be grateful for how your day has gone. For example, I consider any day without an undue level of anxiety or a panic attack to be a good day! Some of my days indeed are better than others, but I always try to enjoy and be grateful for every day without anxiety, no matter what else has happened. Some folks may say I'm settling the bar pretty low; but I beg to differ. This is extremely

important to me, and given this peaceful base of operations, I'm happy to deal with a life that points forward using whatever skills and ability I may have.

> Give yourself positive self-talk 24/7. For starters, tell yourself any or all of the items in this list.

Will your attitude, addiction to perfection, and/or perspective change overnight? Hardly! It has been the work of my lifetime to get to where I am, but it is worth it! What else do you have to do that is more important? I would submit the answer is "Nothing!"

PERSPECTIVE SUPERCHARGES MINDFULNESS

There was a time when it seemed that mindfulness had taken over as the latest and greatest of all self-help techniques. The theory seemed to be that just about anything you could do would be better if done mindfully. This included breathing, eating, exercising, walking, listening, seeing, meditating, etc. It even extended to coloring and tea drinking (no joke – I Googled these.)

While I certainly agree that it has its place, for me it falls short of the be-all and end-all that some see it as. I present my reasoning below and explain why I feel that mindfulness, while powerful in some circumstances, also has limitations. I also say why I think perspective, when added, creates a more powerful tool.

Let me start with some recent definitions of mindfulness:

> Webster's dictionary defines mindfulness as "a mental state achieved by focusing one's awareness on the present moment, while calmly acknowledging and accepting one's feelings, thoughts, and bodily sensations."

> An ad for a mindfulness course featuring Dr. Jon Kabat-Zinn, a guru in the field, offered this definition of mindfulness: "Paying

attention, being on purpose in the present moment, in a non-judgmental way."

> An article in the *New Orleans Advocate* on September 13, 2015, says that mindfulness "...leads you to think about the present and not worry about things beyond your control. We worry about a lot of things we are not able to control. Staying focused on where we are and what we are doing in the moment can help us."

Many, many people today will tell all of us to "live in the moment, be in the moment;" something I consider to be excellent advice from these points of view:

> Avoiding guilt, shame, and regret from living in the past, and
> Avoiding worry, fear, and anxiety from concentrating on the future.

Thus, I agree that mindfulness is indeed an incredibly valuable and powerful tool. The practice of mindfulness also says to accept our feelings and let them be (e.g., when we are sad, we are to be sad). We are not to judge them, fight them, or allow them to control our lives.

I do think mindfulness also deserves a big endorsement when applied to activities like eating; and mindfulness exercises, such as sampling, say, a piece of chocolate or fruit are impactful. As you do so, you are advised to be mindful by eating slowly and tasting the food; to savor it, and really enjoy its attributes. You pay attention! This will not only help you enjoy your food more, but also help you reduce overeating.

But while I am certainly not a mindfulness expert, I personally do not feel it is the best 24/7/365 lifestyle. From my vantage point mindfulness has always been somewhat limited—yet I also understand that my view is certainly not a popular one. It is hard to say anything negative about mindfulness in today's psychological and therapeutic environment; it is the psychological equivalent of being against motherhood and apple pie! And I do not mean to do that.

So why do I feel as I do about the practice of mindfulness? I believe mindfulness is best when supplemented with a strong dose of perspective, gratitude, and empathy for others who may have even harsher circumstances than we do, or for those who are possibly having extreme difficulty handling conditions even less severe. If you employ mindfulness alone— without these other aspects—it might keep you overly focused on yourself and the issues with which you are dealing. Of course, you don't want to ignore or deny how you are really feeling—but perspective, gratitude, and empathy can offer great benefits and help lift the fog more quickly. Adding a dose of perspective to mindfulness can get you back to feelings of gratitude and empathy and assist you in recognizing your blessings more expeditiously than mindfulness alone. You do not want to just stay stuck in the muck of your own situation, right? My view is that perspective can supercharge mindfulness and allow you to get over bumps in the road faster than through simply concentrating on the present.

Here's another way to make the point: Mindfulness tends to keep you from looking forward or backward due to its emphasis on staying in the present moment. On the other hand, perspective is looking up, down, and around. Perspective is *B-R-O-A-D*, whereas an emphasis on mindfulness can be somewhat narrow. It is good for us to see what else is going on; it can help get us out of a narrow personal view. It is more than likely your situation is not so bad when you compare it to that of others (although of course it could be), and you may find it helpful to acknowledge that you are simply getting some of the rain that falls in everyone's life, or that it's just your cosmic turn to have a lousy day! Everyone has a terrible day from time to time, but the less we buy into the negative feelings and pain, the sooner and easier it is for us to rise above them. Recognize a situation for what it is using perspective rather than wallow in bad feelings just because the current moment really is miserable. Too heavy a reliance on mindfulness can be the exact opposite of, and anathema to, perspective; and this can keep us rooted in the unhappiness and negativity that may be our present circumstance.

Those people who accept mindfulness without exception might say that by pushing perspective, gratitude, and empathy as I do, I am being negative or negating how a person feels. That is not my intent. In the sense of actively feeling how we feel and fully experiencing those emotions, I DO believe in mindfulness. We just need to ensure that we don't let the practice of mindfulness put us in the mode of preventing or inhibiting perspective, gratitude, empathy, and so on, which are so very necessary and can help us rise above our current situation.

Being mindful while adding a dose of perspective can keep you both rooted and hopeful. Perspective actually can help keep us sane many times! There are some nasty things going on daily in our world, with terrible things happening to innocent and good people. If we don't keep our wits about us and employ a good sense of perspective, it is difficult, if not impossible, to have a good day and a cheerful outlook.

Despite its good points, mindfulness can, at times, pull us into tragedies, heartache, and pain. So, certainly be mindful of what you are feeling; but be certain to also have the perspective that possibly things aren't quite so bad, could become better, and can be overcome! Employing perspective strikes me as a more stable way to go through the ups and downs and rollercoaster twists and turns of daily life.

As I end this discussion, I would make the related point that excessive mindfulness, or too much emphasis only on what is going on in the moment, can get us in real trouble at times. During two separate times of being one hundred percent in the moment and totally engaged in what I was doing, I had serious accidents. In the first instance I was so totally enthralled with the present-moment thrill of zip-lining that I failed to think ahead enough to lift my feet and use them as shock absorbers to cushion myself against slamming into the side of a rock face. (When I hit that rock, I literally saw stars.)

In the other case, I was so engaged in the excitement of my second solo skydive that I failed to look around and realize where I would be landing...so I didn't maneuver myself away from a reinforced concrete runway to the nearby soft dirt field! The landing shattered my ankle, and only after a lengthy operation and a year of recovery could I walk normally again.

To be clear, whether I was in an emotional pinch or simply dealing with normal daily life, I would use 100% perspective with no mindfulness every time before I would opt for the reverse. However, it is a combination of the two that is optimal!

CHAPTER 14
THE CASE FOR POSITIVE THINKING

"THE GENERAL CONSENSUS is that optimism makes people happier and results in better health outcomes, physical and mental."

- Dr. Clifford, PhD, LCSW, Ochsner Medical Facilities

When it comes to positive thinking and optimism, please do not dismiss this concept or write it off as just being airy-fairy. Some folks believe positive thinking is just some silly, inconsequential gimmick; and while I would have said the same thing when young, I would now say these people are wrong to hold such a belief. From a personal point of view, I know the value in positive thinking is undeniable...and eventually could be a person's salvation!

I have great empathy for these who feel pessimism is a shield for disappointment, and that it is better to be pessimistic and avoid the letdown when things go wrong, as they do from time to time. I actually made this very argument to my dad when I was young and had been asked why I was generally negative (and I was!). But it is now about 70 years later and I'm happy to report that I have been a confirmed optimist for decades.

It is best not to fear disappointment. Rather, take it head on and learn to deal with it! It's just part of life, and we all get our share. But why forgo the incredible benefits of optimism to protect yourself only partially, at best, from the downturns? To me, it doesn't make sense – the math just doesn't work! It is like digging a bomb shelter in your yard and living in the dark 24/7/365 in case there is an attack vs. playing all day with your family and friends in the fresh air and sunshine while acknowledging that someday things may get worse, and being ready if it does.

I had trouble accepting the mantra of positive thinking until motivational author Normal Vincent Peale wrote his bestselling *The Power of*

Positive Thinking . What it contained was revolutionary for me and millions of others! The book supported and also documented the tremendous benefits of optimism. Well over half a century has passed now since that work's original 1952 publication, and with all the incredible leaps that have occurred since in science, medicine, and technology, I think it is now a proven fact that the benefits of a positive mental attitude (PMA) truly exist.

How you think and the foundation from which you proceed in your life makes an enormous difference. Bad things may still happen; but how you deal with them and work through them makes all the difference with your happiness as well as, in some cases, your life and death. There is much evidence already—and more is coming in—that your attitude plays an incredibly important part in many situations.

INFINITELY BETTER

One of the best arguments I have seen about the advantages of a PMA appears in Byron Reese's s book *Infinite Progress*. Mr. Reese writes that a PMA is the foundation of courage—quite an interesting concept —and then goes on to explain the following:

> It is pessimism that says we are doomed. It is pessimism that says why bother? Pessimism is numbing, demoralizing, depressing. Pessimism turns to apathy, which turns to paralysis. Pessimism is all the reasons this will not work. Pessimism hides in the closet fearing the worst. Pessimism quite frankly will get us all killed. Optimism on the other hand says there is a way. Optimism says let's get to work. Optimism is empowering, uplifting, inspiring. Optimism turns into enthusiasm which turns into action. Optimism is 'we will figure out as we go along.' Optimism faces the world hoping for the best. If we have the will and do the work, we can make the world greater than we ever imagined.

It truly is an optimist's world!

WHAT POSITIVE THINKING MANIFESTS

Many top-tier athletes and other highly productive and effective people employ coaches to help them with the effort to be a positive thinker. Psychological literature is replete with the value of positive thinking, with my favorite being an early study done with basketball players trying to improve their foul shot completions. The results showed that those who simply visualized shooting and completing foul shots improved as much those who actually practiced! And what is visualization about successfully achieving a desired goal other than a form of positive thinking?

VISUALIZATION WORKS!

Positive thinking is important not only for athletes but the rest of us. It has been proven that people with a PMA have fewer health and medical issues and improved longevity and are actually happier and more stress-free.

A recent "Today Show" medical report offered yet another good point: Patients with a positive, relaxed attitude and emotional state before their surgery have been shown to have fewer complications versus those who went into a procedure anxious, negative, and/or stressed. The optimist's immune and other systems are better able to deal with the aftermath of surgery than a pessimist's bodily systems that would be somewhat busy dealing with anxiety, stress, and /or a negative outlook.

A positive mental attitude also will let you change your mental reflexes and expand your comfort zones more easily. Positive self-talk and positive thoughts say, "I can do this!" or "I can get through this!" And...

> **As Henry Ford told us, "Whether you think you can, or think you can't, you're right."**

So go ahead...be hopeful and visualize how well things are going to turn out!

HOW BAD IS IT, REALLY?

There are those who support the idea that positive thinking actually manifests what we envision or hope for. Others, however, feel that ours is more of a "what will be will be" world and that thinking positively changes nothing. There is also the reality that positive thinking will not work in all cases (e.g., try thinking positively that if you drop something it will not fall, or in my case, that I can dunk a basketball!) and that we cannot change the laws of physics or certain other constraints or future events.

But what is so important to me is how you and I feel—and positive thinkers feel better, are happier, and are more productive. They are infinitely more likely to achieve their goals than their negative counterparts.

Daniel G. Amen, M.D., has done studies using extensive brain imaging, and he reports that there are changes in a person's brain function when the individual uses optimistic vs. pessimistic thinking. In his book *Change Your Mind, Change Your Life*, Dr. Amen says that positive thinking releases chemicals in the brain which affect a person's reactions, creates lower levels of stress and a slower heart rate, relaxes their breathing, and so on. For these reasons he feels we should train our minds to talk back to our negative thoughts rather than accept them, thereby avoiding the common problem of letting our minds make things seem worse than they really are.

Besides, having a PMA makes not just you but others feel good! My family still jokes at times about "no more caffeine for Dad!" while we are together in a car because of the unfettered joy and wonderment I express on the rides. During our drives to school or work in the mornings (and after a couple of cups of coffee), I would often admire commonplace objects by saying things like "Wow! Look at that tree (or car, or house, etc.)" All of us would laugh at my simplistic childlike enthusiasm—but doing so was, and still is, fun for me and just an expression of joy.

I also believe that judging your position on the continuum between the two extremes of optimism and pessimism is a good measure to take of your progress toward good mental, as well as physical health. I realize there is no generally accepted scale for measuring this, but perhaps you can ask yourself and others whether you come across as a positive can-do type of person or a less positive, negative type.

LET'S HOPE!

Most of us would agree that hope is directly connected to having a positive mental attitude. I would say that the two are almost synonymous—and if you argue they're not, you might still have to admit they are definitely intertwined. For example, when you have hope there is more to live for...and when you have a positive attitude, you feel the same way!

One of my favorite writers for *The Wall Street Journal*, Elizabeth Bernstein, wrote an article in the March 21, 2016, issue concerning the importance of, and need for, hope in our lives. In "An Emotion We All Need More Of," she made the following points:

> Hope is a critical element of our physical and mental well-being. It is a belief that the future will be better than the present, and that you have some power to make it so.

> Those with it [hope] have healthier habits, sleep, and exercise more, eat healthier foods, and even practice safer sex (according to Bernstein's research). They also have fewer colds and less high blood pressure; are more likely to survive cancer; and are less likely to suffer from depression.

> Students with hope have higher grades and are more likely to complete college.

> Couples who have shared hopes are more satisfied with life and their relationships, and their relationships are more likely to last.

> People with hope don't just wish; they are more likely to have a strategy to accomplish their dreams as well as the motivation to implement their plans. You have to work at achieving your goals!

> Hope is contagious, so it is a good idea to spend time with other hopeful people.

> Meditation can help you stay focused on your hopes.

> The more you adopt a positive mental attitude into your life, the less time you spend with defeating thoughts, and the sooner you will leave negativity behind when it bites you.

All the same is true for having a positive mental attitude, and I believe you could substitute "PMA" for the word "hope" every time it appears in the above recap.

SUPERCHARGE A HEALTHY SELF-IMAGE

One of the best and most concise discussions that I have seen on the importance of a good self-image and the need to love yourself is written by John Powell, S. J. in his book *The Christian Vision: The Truth That Sets Us Free*. While he does not specifically tie PMA to a good self-image, I believe it underpins his statements. A slightly edited version of it is included below:

Obviously, if you are seriously under the spell of some of the negative feelings or emotions, it is going to be difficult to be feeling too good about yourself. There are times when a person may be criticized for thinking too highly of him/herself; but it seems to me that the larger problem by far has to do with those who have an unnecessarily low self-image. This may be the result of some negative life experiences, or it might be independent and free-standing. Whatever the cause, the result is a diminished life.... We often do things because of fear vs. freedom – to avoid vs. to achieve ... avoid disappointing others, avoid criticism, being different, losing friends, etc. While there are many causes for fear, many of the things we try to avoid relate to not having a sufficiently strong self-image to feel willing to risk these.

WHY WE ARE SO PESSIMISTIC

To a significant degree we are pessimists by nature. I believe it is in our DNA—literally. Let me explain.

I think that, from a historical or evolutionary perspective, man originally learned to do be pessimistic for survival's sake. When Neanderthal Ned went out for a walk and heard a noise, Ned ended up with a longer life if he assumed the sound belonged to a man-eating saber-toothed tiger rather than a nice cute, cuddly kitty. To illustrate this, let's look at Ned's life expectancy depending on his outlook and actions. If we assume Ned is an optimist and always sees his prehistoric world as being full of playful kittens, he will be fine if this happens to be true in a particular instance. However, if he ends up facing down a saber-toothed tiger, it will probably be bye-bye, Ned! No offspring for you, big guy; and the dinosaurs won't be the only species to become extinct. But if Ned is a bit more cautious and something of a pessimist, he might run and hide at the sound of any animal until he knows more, and thereby live to fight and procreate another day. Put another way, Ned, the adrenaline pumping pessimist, tended to live longer to pass along his DNA more often than his dopamine induced "let's go pet the kitty" friends who were lucky to see the next sunrise.

You might say this is irrelevant ancient history and that we are in the 21st century now; and it is not likely that we are going to encounter many tigers during a normal day. But the 30,000 years since Ned made his exit from the scene represents only the blink of an eye in evolutionary terms. Our brains have not yet adapted to our new lifestyle! So, I believe that we still tend to be pessimists, which causes the very same flight-or-fight emotional thoughts and reactions that kept Ned alive to continue coursing through our systems. But now since we cannot simply run from our stressors, they can cause panic attacks and other emotional issues for us.

I think it can also be said that our survival instinct helps to explain what seems to be a DNA-based dislike for change in humans. Change, after all, is the first sign of DANGER for Ned! And his progeny would not have existed if Ned went skipping through the meadow toward the new dinosaur tracks he just came across.

The dis-ease of all too frequent pessimism no longer serves man today, and it should not come as a surprise to my diligent readers that I believe we can change this attitude! I have done it to a large degree myself, and that's how I know you can too.

JOURNEY TO OPTIMISM

Two stone masons were working on the same structure doing the exact same job in the exact same overbearing heat. When the first is asked what he is doing, he said he just keeps putting stones in place, one after another, and that he sees himself as doing hard, repetitive labor out in the hot sun. When the second mason is asked the same question, he sits back briefly, looking up to the top of the structure, and replies that he is building a cathedral as a tribute to God.

Now ask yourself, which man feels better when he gets home at night? Which man do you suppose has a happier life? And which man is more likely to stick with the job longest and live longest?

If you're not a PMA advocate yet, please know the important thing is to begin the journey and then to stay with it while thinking positively and with hope. Sure, things do not go well in every case for anyone; we all experience disappointments and failures. Yet when you look at all the benefits of having a positive mental attitude, it's clear to me that the pursuit of a PMA is the best and most reasonable and effective approach to take in life.

Back in my 20's I had an epiphany about the benefits of having a positive mental attitude, in terms of looking at the glass half full vs. half empty. I used to go home every night from work thinking about what I had not gotten done, what was not completed, and all I had to do the next day. As if the stress and pressures of the day weren't bad enough, I just piled more and more of it on myself!

It finally dawned on me to look at the other side of the coin: I began thinking in as much detail as possible about all I had DONE during the day—what I had accomplished or completed, what I had moved along, and the progress I had made across different fronts. Nothing actually changed in terms of what had been accomplished and what was left to do; but I can honestly say the change in attitude and perspective made a tremendous difference in how I felt. Eventually doing this became a habit, and I was much more relaxed, enthused, and happy when I got home from work. This had a major positive effect on my family life.

In a way, this is very much like the effect you get from meditation or other self-help strategies. The world and universe do not change during these activities; the change that has taken place is between your ears! This is the place where our stress and anxiety live. You can look out into the world, but you'll never see stress or anxiety per se; they are not dark clouds that envelop you. It all stems from your attitude and your mental conditioning.

At the end of the day, pessimistic thinking detracts from the peace and happiness you can enjoy in life, to say nothing of the effect on your creativity or your way of reacting to different circumstances that arise. As Charlie Brown once noted:

> **"Worrying won't stop the bad stuff from happening; it just keeps you from enjoying the good."**

-Wisdom from *Peanuts!*

———◆———

IS IT POSSIBLE TO BE AN OPTIMIST IN TODAY'S WORLD?

Today's times are tough; there are violent protests, assaults, intolerance, cruelty, the degradation of our environment, the destruction of our planet, normal fears about war, the additional concern regarding the possibility of nuclear war, and no end of examples of man's inhumanity to man. Because the world is so connected these days due to the advances in technology, many of us also are seeing an almost non-stop stream of stories about terrible things that have occurred halfway across the world. Upholding a PMA in the face of all this can be a challenge.

So let me provide you with some excellent examples of why we can be proud and happy about what we have accomplished in the past and why we are very justified in being optimistic about man's future.

First, in *The Better Angels of Our Nature*, author Steven Pinker makes an incredibly powerful and convincing case that the world is actually getting less violent these days—in stark contrast to what most of us feel after the daily news broadcasts! We tend to forget, ignore, or be unaware of how truly horrendous the wars, destruction, and pestilence have been historically, as far back as our earliest history. He feels there is good reason to think the situation will continue to improve further.

In the book *Infinite Progress*, Byron Reese lays out a very compelling case for the real benefits humankind is bringing to the world:

> The end of hunger, war, poverty, and other social issues can at least be imagined at this time. Many felt they were intractable and would always be with us.

> Health advances and medical breakthroughs with DNA sequencing and other new medical technologies across almost all aspects of the healing arts.

> Better educational opportunities available to all on the web and/ or in the classroom.

> Supercomputers helping with medical diagnoses, and phones or watches allowing for remote access to health care and testing.

> Artificial intelligence advances.

> Clean water for all.

> Cheaper alternate sources of electricity and the use of electric cars all resulting in reduced emissions.

> 3-D printing and related technologies to help develop prosthetic limbs, etc. that benefit people who are suffering or disabled.

> Safer self-driving cars with fewer accidents and less damage or injury when an accident does happen.

> The great economic benefits of the microloans and agricultural advances for third world countries.

> And so many other positive trends.

When we consider some of our accomplishments as a society and the positive effects we are beginning to have on the world and its inhabitants, it certainly should bring a smile to your face and hope to your mind!

So yes, we are magnificent in many ways, although we have a very long way to go before we even remotely reach our potential and the highest ideals to which we might aspire. Yet I love the fact that we are still TRYING! This is the fundamental requirement.

DON'T GO ALL MARY POPPINS ON ME

Optimism can be overdone, however! And if this happens to you, you will be unprepared for what is and will be happening in your life. The term "cockeyed optimist" is therefore justifiable and signifies an over-reliance on the Good Fairy. In our daily lives it would be unfortunate if we started acting like Mary Poppins will come to transform our lives and that everything will somehow work out. We need to be realistic too! Not all hopes can be achieved, no matter how strong the wish, how detailed the strategy and planning, or how strong the motivation.

An article in *The Wall Street Journal* titled "A Perfect Dose of Pessimism" by Sumathi Reddy suggests it is best to have a balance of optimism and pessimism... weighted towards optimism. I would tweak this to say the best mix is between optimism and realism. In my opinion, this is rational, productive, efficient, and motivating.

CONCLUSION ON THE PMA ADVANTAGE

To recap the advantages of a PMA, let me simply present the following concerning what a PMA provides:

>A more enjoyable, freer life with stronger personal bonds and better relationships

>Higher productivity

>Better mental and physical health

>A more realistic life

To end this section, let me offer you the quote from a small plaque I have in my closet:

> **"In the kingdom of hope there is no winter."**

For me, this says it all!

PART III

SPECIFIC STRATEGIES – TRAINING THE MIND

PART III - OVERVIEW

THE NEXT THREE PARTS of the book include the strategies I developed, discovered, or learned from others. Regardless of their source, I have used every single one of them and found them helpful in various situations, whether it was aiding me to become less anxious and stressed, or allowing me to see there were options available when my feet were in the quicksand of depression.

This first part deals with strategies to help calm your mind completely on your own. No interaction with others is involved with these. Part IV concerns getting out into the world and interacting with others. Part V includes other actions or choices you can make to improve your life and attain greater peace.

Some of these strategies may sound simplistic to you, and they well may be. But just because an idea is simple doesn't mean it isn't useful, helpful, or extremely worthwhile. Trust me, you will encounter others which are much more challenging!

One thing that never fails to impress me is that something which is easy for one person can be excruciatingly difficult for another, and vice versa. To paraphrase Abraham Lincoln:

> **Some of the strategies are for all the people.**
> **All of the strategies are for some of the people.**
> **But all of the strategies are not for all the people.**

Use the strategies that work for you, set aside those that don't. And please don't worry about the category into which I have put a particular strategy. The category is not important; the strategy is what counts.

Also, you may be aware that there are books, bookstores full of books, and even entire libraries devoted to some of the particular strategies included here. I am not trying to summarize everything about each strategy or technique in order to compete with the other works; no one person can do all of that. I simply want to make some points about the aspects that have resonated with me and worked for me.

My hope is that the strategies I've selected here will jumpstart you on your own journey. If these strategies work to eliminate or somewhat reduce the problems and symptoms you experience, sometimes that is the most that can be done.

Remember: if you have a problem, but having the problem is NOT a problem, then you really don't have a problem! And that's good news indeed.

So, let's have a look at the strategies.

CHAPTER 15
DO NOT FEAR MIND CONTROL

A TERM THAT STRIKES almost universal fear and loathing in the minds of most people is "mind control." Just think of any of the following:

> Subliminal advertising
> George Orwell's book *1984*
> The movie "The Manchurian Candidate"

Did you grimace upon reading those references? Well, please permit me to give you another way to look at mind control so that your physical (and emotional) reaction can be extremely different. What I am talking about is our own control over our own minds. Internal mind control is quite a good thing, for the more we can be in control of our minds and focus them on what we want to accomplish, the more peace, positivity, and happiness we can achieve. After all:

> **What is a panic attack but a mind that is out of control?**

Let's face it, many mental health issues such as excessive fear, anxiety, stress, guilt, or shame really represent and originate from the mind being out of control or not functioning in its normal manner. In such cases the mind races or ruminates with negative thoughts and emotions, resulting in the person whose mind it is suffering from what feels like the torments of hell!

When people experience the negative effects of excessive and debilitating thoughts, generally what they want the most is to get the mind back under control. They wish, hope, and pray just to be normal. I know I did!

Granted, training your mind to think what you want it to will affect how and what you think; but your thinking is the whole problem, right? From this point of view, exercising mind control on yourself is the ultimate goal! You are in charge and you decide what your thoughts are. This is different from where you may be now.

The more time and effort you take to train your mind to be relaxed, at peace, grateful, and optimistic, the less time your mind—and by extension, you—will be uptight and anxious. Said another way:

> **The more you rid yourself of negative feelings and emotions, the more you and your mind can spend in a peaceful state, and in your happy place.**

Finally, looking at the topic from the other end of the telescope, if you cannot control your mind, what chance do you have for happiness, relaxation, gratitude, and productivity? Your mind could take you to horrible places, never slow down, never concentrate, and achieve little or no peace or productivity. To me, this is hell; and I prefer to never return!

***

TECHNIQUES FOR TRAINING YOUR MIND

Much of exercising control over your mind will be a matter of both choice and practice. I have been in situations in which I would have given anything just to be able to calm my mind, and I fully understand that at a given moment you may not be able to exercise this control to your own satisfaction. But I still defend the use of the word "choice" because I believe for most of us there are strategies that we can practice and improve on greatly over time to achieve this mastery. But we must choose to do the work!

Even deciding to practice is a choice! Of course, we could argue that chemical substances in the brain may be beyond the effects of simple practice, but I believe the vast majority of anxiety issues can be helped by practice. We have all heard of people who can handle what seem like impossible conditions, rise above them, and find peace, forgiveness, love, and/or gratitude. We are all capable of moving in that direction.

As a conclusion to this section, consider these quotes confirming the benefits of training your mind to listen to YOU from two famous Americans:

> **Your own mind is a sacred enclosure into which nothing harmful can enter except by your promotion.**

~ Ralph Waldo Emerson

I would amend this slightly to add acquiescence, permission, or lack of diligence.

Next, in the words of another great American, Eleanor Roosevelt:

> **It's your life - but only if you make it so.**

This is a brief chapter and is meant to simply introduce the concept of expanding your control over your own mind. Many specifics are included in the remaining chapters and in the LOU's.

CHAPTER 16
STRATEGY - LIVE IN A STATE OF GRATITUDE

THERE ARE VERY FEW mental outlooks that can provide the benefits that come with a genuinely grateful attitude.

You may have to work at achieving a lasting state of gratitude, but I believe that this strategy alone, as it is mastered, will greatly reduce anxiety issues, depression, shame, rage, bitterness, jealousy, greed, stress, and more! It certainly does that for me, although it has been a lifetime effort to progress as far as I have to date. I can tell you, however, that every bit of effort that has gone into achieving this progress is worth it.

I don't know about you, but I simply can't be filled with gratitude and discontent at the same time. Gratitude brings peace; and for me, peace dispels anxiety, sadness, and anger every time!

> **If you can maintain it, gratitude is a tremendous help in reducing negative emotions and thoughts.**

You may remember I said above that some of the strategies may seem easy to master but others would be more difficult? Well, this is one that can be challenging. The good news is that it is all up to you – it is within your control. It is that simple. Here are some thoughts to help:

> Gratitude isn't really complicated; certainly, it's not rocket science.

> The tricky part of gratitude is not to understand what it is conceptually. The tricky part is to stay with it 24/7/365.

> I'm sure we have all experienced gratitude, but then we move on to something else or get dragged back into the frustrations, etc., of daily life.

> I believe that maintaining a state of gratitude is doable … but it takes reminding yourself of why you should be grateful and practicing gratitude time after time until it becomes as natural as breathing.

> Can you even IMAGINE feeling grateful all or most of the time? Wouldn't that be fantastic? Use that feeling as motivation to achieve this goal.

> Feeling grateful provides one of our warmest and most wonderful experiences!

> **Always keep trying and practicing! The more you do it, the better life gets.**

For more specific and granular suggestions, you may like to consider these:

> Use *The Greatest Miracle* by Og Mandino as a place to start. It puts great emphasis on being grateful.

> Employ daily affirmations or engage in daily meditation that focuses on being grateful and identifies your blessings.

> Start a gratitude journal, including within it: your meaningful thoughts; personal stories; anecdotes which helped you experience and/or feel gratitude; and sayings or quotes from other people that are meaningful to you in this regard.

> Think of those who love you—family and friends as well as your pets and others. Think enjoyable thoughts.

> You will never have this day with your children and other loved ones again; tomorrow, they'll be a little older than they were today. The day is a gift; breathe it in. And then, as Dr. Seuss says: "Don't be sad it is over, be grateful that it happened."

> See the discussion on perspective above; perspective and gratitude are highly interlinked.

CHAPTER 17
STRATEGY - APPRECIATE THE DISCOMFORT

I HAVE A QUESTION FOR you:

> **Can you envision yourself ever being grateful for the issues that have plagued you?**

I can tell you that when I was in the middle of dealing with my own issues, my answer would have been a resounding "NO!" But to be honest, that is not my answer today.

While feeling and believing this may be a stretch for almost all of us, I do believe there is something to be grateful for concerning any mental discomfort: It is the body's way of telling us that something is out of whack. The discomfort or disturbance is a warning system that there is something wrong that requires our attention and/or that we may have violated a part of our value system. Very possibly something is inconsistent in our way of handling life and the many situations that arise in that process.

There is something good about these disturbances, and that's where gratitude can come in: They provide a good deal of motivation to understand and correct our thinking and actions in various ways. If we act on this motivation, it can lead to HUGE positive changes in our lives. We can choose to handle particular situations differently in the future, and we can become better people.... more proficient and attuned to reality.

ANGER TELLS US A LOT

A more specific example of a feeling we have that might ordinarily be thought of as a negative but which we can learn to be grateful for are feelings of anger. Someone once observed that anger for another affects us like we are swallowing poison: It turns out worse for us than the target of our anger (Mark Goulston MD, *Talking to Crazy*). The best approach is to rid ourselves of anger whenever possible.

However, we can learn a lot about ourselves by examining what makes us angry. For example, I do not often get mad at people, but when I do, I know I should see what is really behind my emotions. The triggers I identify can lead to important understandings about myself, reinforce those concepts or aspects, or make it clear that I need to make changes in a relationship, etc. In my case, when I was young, I was on the wrong end of many unfair fights with my older brother; and it still can make me angry to this day to see mismatched fights among others (e.g., people of power, physical strength, celebrity status, etc. taking advantage of others who are lacking in these.) Fortunately, I have developed many ways of dealing with that anger, because it can be unbelievably bad to keep these feelings bottled up. Anger has been shown to be injurious to us physically and medically (think higher blood pressure and more adrenaline) and it is a crippling, detrimental, isolating way to live over the long term.

The main point here is that even though experiences of guilt, shame, rage, regret, and so on are not enjoyable in and of themselves, perhaps we can learn from them to internalize more humility, empathy, and gratitude. And here's an interesting way to do just that: Think of negative feelings as though they are people, and work to both forgive them and thank them. Many are just trying to help you, protect you, improve you, defend you, teach you new lessons, and help you cope with situations in the only way they know how.

⎯⎯●⎯⎯

DISCOMFORT SETS US APART

Actually, feelings of anxiety, guilt, or regret are a part of mankind's nobility: They set us apart from all other animals. Think of cats and how they act. As much as I love cats, I don't think they ever feel bad about killing a mother bird and leaving the babies on their own to survive. Nor do dogs really feel bad when they eat our sofas. They have no thoughts of guilt or remorse and they do not strive to be better pets.

Most of us, on the other hand, WOULD feel differently if we acted as a dog or cat does. Our experiences of negative emotions can give us an impetus to change and do better; to become more capable and empathetic.

> ### Emotional issues can become steppingstones which make growth possible.

In fact, the amount of gratitude we can (or don't) feel for our adversities is a benchmark by which we can assess our current status and progress to date. In my own case, I have come to appreciate the struggles I have had with anxiety as I would not be the person I am today without them. I would be quite different—far from as understanding and empathetic as I am now. For me, empathy, understanding, and the desire to help others have all come from my own issues, to say nothing of my greatly increased understanding and acceptance of myself. My gifts have been many as a result of my trials, tribulations, and the path I have travelled.

All of us with struggles can choose to focus on and appreciate what we have learned and how much we have grown since our attempts at self-improvement began. But I definitely would like to help you find a gentler and more compassionate road to these lessons than I had at first! Learn to pat yourself on the back, sit back, and savor your progress. Look at what you have learned and appreciate how you have grown as a result.

Difficult times bring good things more often than we think.

CHAPTER 18

STRATEGY - EXPAND COMFORT ZONES ... DO IT ANYWAY!

"A ship is safe in the harbor, but that's not what ships are for."

- Wm. G. T. Shedd, American Theologian (1820-1894).

ANXIETY, PANIC, AND stress often occur when we get to the end of what we consider to be our comfort zone. We can't be anxious and simultaneously be within our comfort zone, right? So, to stay relaxed, productive, positive, and on something of an even keel, it makes sense to enjoy the widest or largest possible comfort zones.

Just think about it: What if we were comfortable in any and all situations? Manna from heaven, right? The good news is that comfort zones can function in the same way rubber bands do: They can be stretched to become larger and more flexible, making us better able to go with the flow so we can be more comfortable engaging in new experiences and taking appropriate risks.

***

WAYS TO GROW

I know of three effective ways to expand our comfort zones:

1. Continue to live life, accumulating experiences and thereby expanding your comfort zones at the normal pace. For example, some people who have never travelled to a foreign country might be nervous about doing so ... but having done so once, chances are that they will be much more comfortable the next time.

2. Before taking on something new, study what is normal and to be expected in terms of a new situation or event in which you might find yourself. There is no need to wait for life to happen and only

then reinvent the wheel, so to speak. You can read, learn, and grow from studying. This can lessen a blow that life might otherwise deliver. To use our previous example of international travel: If you learn some words and phrases likely to be helpful in the country to which are you planning to travel, it can reduce your stress once you arrive and are travelling there.

3. INTENTIONALLY do things that fall outside of your comfort zones. For instance, select some physical activity (e.g., a five-mile run? Bodybuilding? Learning to ski or snowboard?) that challenges your strength or courage. Or do something that you know you are not good at or comfortable with, like offering to run a workshop even though you are nervous about speaking publicly.

Most of us have a normal "I don't want to embarrass myself" reaction when certain activities are suggested ... but it is incredibly freeing to defy these and do things anyway just for the fun of it! Get out on the dance floor when you are not a good dancer and shake your booty, or do anything like the following ... all of which I really am glad I have tried:

- Get out on an NBA basketball court during halftime and do a dance routine with others. I do not consider myself a particularly good dancer in general, so for me this was risking the embarrassment of all embarrassments. I probably practiced 20 hours in advance for what would be a 2-minute routine and never got it down perfectly, but the experience turned out to be glorious. The crowd was wonderfully supportive and appreciative. Also, while I had assumed no one I knew would see or recognize me, I was busted by a neighbor, who happens to be a Federal Judge, on my way back to my car! And to further test my capacity for embarrassment, I found a video of the performance waiting for me when I got to the office the next day; it had been circulated to everyone in the office already. But it turned out to be wonderful: We all had many good laughs, and I could feel the friendship and support.

- Take up yoga. When I thought of myself trying to do yoga before I signed up for the class, it seemed as logical an endeavor as trying to teach a water buffalo to do ballet or to push a ton of Jell-O up a tree trunk! However, I stayed with the classes for over a year, and I found yoga freeing and enjoyable. Every time I left a yoga class I felt better and lighter. It didn't matter that, when I looked around the room, I saw all these lean, lithe, and supple bodies splayed all over the floor; and yet my body happened to be one of the least flexible and most mesomorphic bodies God has ever created. (Thinking of myself in a yoga class is one way I know that God truly has a sense of humor.) But learning yoga was great, and I could almost feel my comfort zone widening as I did so. It is a source of pride and good feelings, and I honestly laugh every time I think of attending classes. Also, yoga is a unique blend of exercise and meditation, and I may well return to it in the future.

- I was once given an assignment by a therapist to do something that seemed really silly to me and which I would absolutely never ordinarily do. It was close to Mardi Gras in New Orleans, and he challenged me to wear a Mardi Gras mask on a normal business day while walking the five blocks from where I parked to my office building. Well, it was actually fun and amusing to see the looks and smiles I got as I strolled to work. I even got a few thumbs-up! No one thought less of me for doing this, and the world certainly did not come to an end. I should acknowledge, however, that probably no one could tell who the masked man was, but you would be surprised at how hard this was anyway.

- Becoming a ball boy (or girl, for my female readers) at a USTA professional tennis event. I had fun doing this although I was just a little disappointed when the special award I had envisioned at the end of the tournament for the "oldest ball boy ever" did not materialize. Go figure!

- Skydiving—after learning to pack my own chute and do proper parachute landing falls, I jumped completely by myself.
- Repelling off a mountain face.

- Zip lining.
- Bungee jumping.

What I managed to accomplish here with what I considered "out-there" activities was to greatly expand my comfort zones. What can you try today that perhaps intrigues you, makes you a bit shy, or makes you nervous?

As bestselling author and actor Neale Donald Walsch has said,

> **"Life begins at the end of your comfort zone."**

Take this to heart!

GO FOR IT!

CHAPTER 19

STRATEGY – BOUNCE BACK QUICKLY THROUGH MENTAL ELASTICITY

IF YOU HAVE STUDIED economics, you have probably heard of price elasticity. This gives an indication of the effect on supply or demand of changes in price, up or down. And if, like me, you have aged beyond a certain point in life, you have probably come in contact with the term "skin elasticity."

Now we all know, unfortunately, that "stuff happens" in life with upsetting things occurring for each and every one of us. The best we can realistically hope for is to handle complex, traumatic, and/or stressful issues well when they are presented, and to bounce back quickly afterwards. With this in mind, I think we can all agree that we want to work towards having the highest possible degree of "mental elasticity."

Mental elasticity, or a mental recovery rate, operates in a fashion similar to a cardiac recovery rate. In medicine or science, we can measure a person's cardiac recovery rate based on how quickly the heart rate returns to normal after exertion. Mental elasticity is the time it takes a person to regain (recover) their normal mental equilibrium after a potentially upsetting event.

With both kinds of recovery, a fast recovery rate is optimal: A shorter time indicates a healthier condition in the person involved. When it comes to a cardiac recovery rate, a person can exercise to help improve that rate. But can you do the same for a mental recovery rate? Well, while you could conjure up specific upsetting events and situations to contemplate and try to work through mentally, I'm not sure it is necessary to stress yourself intentionally in hopes of learning to better control life events. Life will generally take care of that without any help from us. Here's what I recommend in lieu of doing this to heighten your awareness and work toward improving:

> As objectively as possible, try to evaluate your mental elasticity now to serve as a good benchmark that you can use to evaluate yourself over time. Hopefully, as time marches on and you become better able to deal with the situations life has in store for you, your mental elasticity and recovery rate will improve. When this happens, you will know enough to recognize your progress, and therefore be able to recognize and celebrate your improvement and your faster return to normal after an upsetting experience.

> Just raise your awareness of the existence of mental elasticity. It's comforting in and of itself to realize that we all have this trait, and that we all face issues from which we want to bounce back.

In a way your mental elasticity is an overall metric for your success in using any and all practices you follow in order to achieve calm, peace, and stability. It can be a very rewarding experience to smoothly go through a situation that previously would have been very difficult, and to see the progress!

CHAPTER 20
STRATEGY – DEVELOP AFFIRMATIONS

ROUGHLY 40 YEARS AGO someone explained to me the benefits of developing and employing positive affirmations. Affirmations support the practice of having a positive mental attitude (PMA), and an effective way to begin developing that PMA is to develop affirmations, which are statements that reveal your goals, aspirations, and dreams.

In making any list of affirmations for yourself, dream BIG!!! Put your goals in positive terms that let you focus on having already achieved them. The visualization and expression of your goals by speaking or thinking them creates positive thoughts in your mind. This puts you exactly where you want to be mentally and emotionally—and many people believe that this practice helps you create the goal you seek.

It is absolutely fine if one or more goals are not even in sight yet. Some of mine were originally so "not available to me now" when I began the practice that I would usually laugh when I repeated them to myself. But as time went on and changes took place, these became very satisfying because I could see the advances I had made, and the actual accomplishments achieved.

My best example of this is my affirmation that claims the following: "I really enjoy being out of town." You have to understand that travel was the bane of my existence at the time, and I had experienced some of the worst times of my life when out of town for work or on vacation! Now, however, the affirmation is realistic because of my progress, and I get a feeling of amazing peace and gratitude when I say it aloud. I know deep down what I have accomplished here, and it makes me believe I can reach the same state of accomplishment with my other affirmations!

I have actually had times when my anxiety level was simply too high for me to sit down or do what is, in essence, almost any simple activity. But now I am able to say my affirmations when my panicked feelings are just building. For me, the practice of using affirmations has provided an efficient way to relax myself in normal times, return myself to breathing in a proper manner (something which I often could not do while in the midst of a panic attack), and/or to put myself to sleep. The practice of using affirmations has been invaluable for me, so I recommend that you try it.

PUTTING AFFIRMATIONS INTO PRACTICE

Your list of affirmations doesn't have to be tremendously long: I began with only 5 positive thoughts, adding others over the years. I now have 32 and have them listed below in the order I added them.

But having only one affirmation is just fine! For example, you can choose to use only one during meditation, and an affirmation repeated multiple times can have its advantages. Conversely, compiling a longer list has its place too, and a number of affirmations can cover more ground in a person's life. (Since I have over 30, you might correctly surmise that I had a lot of ground to cover!)

It can be extremely helpful to run thorough affirmations while exercising, going to sleep, or as a form of meditation. Feel free to review them aloud or just repeat them in your mind; whatever makes you feel better.

Whatever your affirmations are and however many they number, repeat them daily, trying to build up to 15-20 minutes of solid time during which you are concentrating on the affirmations with feelings of calm and peace. And don't forget to make the wording of any affirmation positive! It is far better to express a positive message about success rather than create and put forth an affirmation that speaks to not failing. Finally, remember that this is not a speed exercise. Say them at a pace that lets your mind concentrate on each one. I found that if I raced through them as quickly as possible, I got no benefit; it encouraged my mind to actually spin faster and move me away from the calm and peace I wanted to achieve.

MY LIST TODAY

To give you examples of what I personally find helpful, I have included below my current list of affirmations. While your list will be very different, as it will be unique to you, you may find mine to be helpful to see the breadth I covered and the variety of sources from which my affirmations came.

1. I am calm, confident, relaxed, and enthusiastic. (A personal goal)
2. I will do everything today that can reasonably be accomplished. (A personal goal)
3. At night I easily relax and go to sleep - whether I am at home or out of town - and wake up in the morning feeling relaxed and well rested. (A personal goal)
4. I really enjoy being out of town. (A personal goal)
5. I generally eat only what is good for my body, and I eat in moderation so that, over a reasonable period of time, I will lose weight and be trimmer. (A personal goal)
6. I am a whole and complete person, and I can be happy and at peace completely on my own. (A personal goal)
7. It never has to be that way again! (Something a friend told me)
8. Touch me, dear Lord, with your peace; and help my troubled mind to know that you are God and I need fear no evil. (Dr. Norman Vincent Peale)
9. The light of God surrounds me, the love of God enfolds me, the power of God protects me, and the presence of God watches over me. Wherever I am, God is, and all is well. (James D. Freeman, Unity Church)
10. Count your blessings, proclaim your rarity, go the extra mile, use wisely your power of choice, do all things with love for yourself, for others and for God. (*Greatest Miracle* by Og Mandino.)
11. I am responsible for what I see; I choose the feelings I experience; and I decide upon the goals I would achieve. And everything that seems to happen to me I ask for and receive as I have asked. (*Course in Miracles*)
12. The peace of God is my one goal. (*Course in Miracles*)
13. I need not wait an instant longer to be at peace forever. (*Course in*

Miracles, Lesson #355)

14. I can see peace instead of this. (*Course in Miracles*, Lesson #341)

15. There is a place inside of me where there is a perfect peace. (*Course in Miracles*, Lesson #47)

16. The mind that serves the spirit is at peace and filled with joy. (*Course in Miracles*, Lesson #96)

17. Forgiveness offers everything I want. (*Course in Miracles*, Lesson #122)

18. All things are lessons God would have me learn. (*Course in Miracles*, Lesson #193)

19. I will be still an instant and go home. (*Course in Miracles*, Lesson #182)

20. I place the future in the hands of God. (*Course in Miracles*, Lesson #194)

21. In fearlessness and love I spend the day. (*Course in Miracles*, Lesson #310)

22. The sounds of love don't just happen; you have to make them. (Radio ad in the '60s - Church of Jesus Christ of the Latter-Day Saints)

23. To know that love is all there is, is all there is to know. (Bumper sticker)

24. I am among the ministers of God. (*Course in Miracles*)

25. To those leaning on the sustaining infinite, today is big with blessings. (A favorite quote from Christian Science, which I heard originally from the patriarch of the family I worked with)

26. May God fill you with peace this day and every day of your life. (Father Arceneaux's blessing at Manresa)

27. I shall not fear the terror of the night nor the arrow that flies by day. (Ps. 91:5)

28. What time I am afraid, I will trust in thee. (A favorite quote of mine from Christian Science)

29. Having done all, stand. (From the Bible - I first heard it from my mother)

30. You are loved (by God); there is nothing to fear. (*Proof of Heaven* by Eban Alexander III)

31. If you knew what God wanted you to do, you would do it and be happy. You are doing what God wants you to do; be happy! (From the "est" training offered in the '60s and later)

32. Not my circus; not my monkeys. (Old Polish proverb)

Now that you are fully aware of my list of affirmations ... what's yours? There are extremely few things to think about and work on that are more important than improving yourself and ridding yourself of negative emotions and thoughts that impede your life. This work constitutes an A-1 priority regardless of almost anything else with which you deal in life. All else will follow if you pay attention to this strategy. As you succeed in ridding yourself of destructive or negative thoughts, actions, or feelings, peace will come.

CHAPTER 21
STRATEGY – PEACE AND RELAXATION THROUGH MEDITATION

PEOPLE HAVE ENJOYED meditation for thousands of years, so its benefits are well known. Not only have millions worldwide in both the present and the past experienced them, but as of late, those benefits have been documented and scientifically demonstrated through modern technology such as brain imaging and other methods. The known benefits include:

> Stress reduction – The body constantly reacts negatively to life's stressors, so living with chronic stress can be very detrimental to all aspects of a person's life.

> Lower blood pressure – The calming effects of meditation can reduce the high blood pressure the body experiences at stressful points in a person's day.

> Better sleep – Going to bed in a more relaxed state can give a person a deeper, longer, more rejuvenating night's rest.

> Less depression – Depression or sadness often worsens if a person dwells on their negative thoughts. Learning how to refocus on the positives using meditation often helps put people in better control of their emotions.

> Lower psychological barriers: Meditation allows people to approach and deal with the traumas of their past and the residual

issues that still exist, according to *Transforming Trauma* by James Finley and Carolyn Myss.

———◉———

MEDITATION AND OTHER PRACTICES

Every single day, each of us lives in what could be called an emotional soup. There are many, many facets to our personalities; and we have emotions and self-judgments floating around simultaneously in our minds. This in turn can create any number of emotions and/or stresses within us, depending on which come to the surface to form conscious feelings. The beauty of meditation is that it focuses and centers the mind and our emotions in a positive way.

In a sense, meditation is an early form of biofeedback. Both techniques train the mind to affect the body and teach a person how to control certain physical feelings and muscle reactions. However, meditation is more for mind control and calming, whereas biofeedback can help us learn to control certain physical and muscle activities.

Also, while some might think meditation and affirmations are essentially the same kind of practice, there are significant differences. Meditations are more general while affirmations tend to be more limited, rifle-shot points. Meditations tend to encompass your whole life and body, while affirmations are more geared to specific facets, goal setting, developing a positive attitude and other traits.

However, when done well, both these practices can help you relax your body and mind. And both benefit from deep, relaxed breathing.

———◉———

TIPS FOR MEDITATING

Here's some advice for those of you who are beginners at meditation. They may also prove helpful to those who have meditated before, but have not done so focusing on the issues and goals in their lives:

> Add a meditation app to your phone so that it goes where you go. The Headspace app is great and takes its users through

a very good program of daily meditations. I also recommend the meditation app Calm.

> Try as many different forms of meditation as you feel might possibly help. You can find a sizable number of methods and links simply by googling on the internet. Keep trying until you determine the ones you like best and whittle down the field.

> Repetition is important. Going through the meditation process on a regular, repetitive, and frequent basis helps a person remember the lessons and lets them sink in more deeply. Also, from time to time, as a person repeats the meditations, nuances that they had not considered before may arise.

> Try a guided meditation in which you listen to someone talking and leading you through the process. This meditation can be live, recorded, online, etc. ... and the speaker can be you, a friend, a spouse, or another trusted person. The idea behind it is that you relax and concentrate on the meditation being offered. A guided meditation takes you through the process without your needing to think or remember anything.

MY PREFERENCE – A TAILORED GUIDED MEDITATION

One of the reasons I personally prefer the guided meditation rather than the type in which you are encouraged to empty your mind of all thoughts is that I was never successful with the latter; it always seemed somewhat unnatural to me, almost as if I were trying to swim upstream! Humans' minds generally work well with visualizations—it is one of the mind's great strengths—and they resist being emptied.

On the other hand, engaging in the practice of guided meditations came naturally to me; I had no difficulty following along and becoming immersed. In fact, once when I was doing a guided meditation led by another person, we got close to the end and it was time to return to the real world and end the mediation, I mentioned that I did not want to come back. The other person, seemingly surprised and possibly alarmed, asked me why. I said, "Why would

I want to come back? This was my favorite place in the universe and many good things were going on in the meditation. Who would want to return?"

Another reason I like guided meditations is that they let me cover as many topics as I choose. And I tend to be a "more is better" person.

Of course, you should meditate in a way that resonates with YOU! Don't get hung up on a particular technique if you continue to struggle with it.

> After you've researched, listened to, and taken part in some guided meditations, consider crafting your own meditation that brings about the state you most desire, whether it is one of peace, joy, hopefulness, or relaxation. Include in your meditation special customized features or symbols meaningful to you. These could include any, or more likely all, of the following:

- People or avatars representing those who have been significant and meaningful to you. There are often loved ones (alive or departed), mentors, role models, and/or animals which have characteristics you admire.
- Your favorite or special place...a place in which you find enjoyment, peace, relaxation, and happiness.
- An activity you really enjoy or find especially relaxing.
- Your favorite time of day.
- All of your senses – perhaps bring in the colors, smells, tastes, touch, and sounds that you associate with all of the above points in this list. So, for example, if your favorite places are the mountains, you might include green fields, blue skies, softly flowing streams, the odor of the forest, the sound of birds, etc.

> Record any guided meditation you craft in your own voice (or have a significant other record it in their own voice), then put it on your cellphone so that it is pretty much always available to you. Let it guide you through the mental process that you want to embed. Again, the idea is that you relax and concentrate on the meditation and let it take you through the process with minimal effort on your part.

There is a basic guided meditation I first heard over ten years ago, and while I've made many changes to it since, I have included it as Appendix B in case it is of interest to you. For your convenience, I have indicated the specific pieces I've added to personalize it for myself. You can easily see where you may like to make some modifications to better suit your own personal situation. You will want to personalize the meditation to include your specifics and the goals you want to achieve, so absolutely feel free to add, delete, or change it in any way to tailor it and make it your own.

CHAPTER 22
STRATEGY – SPIRITUALITY

OBVIOUSLY, THE SPIRITUAL side of life is not for all people; but it became a powerful force for me, someone who did not grow up in a spiritual or religious environment. I had been raised by parents who were wonderful people but who were basically atheists. While even today I certainly would not describe myself as religious, I also doubt anyone has prayed more fervently than I have while in the midst of a panic or major anxiety attack. All I wanted during those episodes was just to be normal!

It was when I reached my 20's that I first started observing the peace, acceptance, and will to persevere that deeply held spiritual beliefs brought to many people I met or knew. For example, I encountered people in the hospital awaiting serious operations, or others who were in the temporal world with turmoil swirling all around them, and yet they were—and remained—serene, happy, and at peace! It was this kind of demonstration that piqued my interest in learning more about spirituality and related beliefs.

I can remember thinking to myself, "I want some of that ... the peace that can come from deep spiritual beliefs!" And so I began trying to internalize the "peace that passes all understanding."

If you are not currently spiritual, could you be open to spirituality and its potential benefits?

SPIRITUAL BLESSINGS
Spiritual beliefs can help with:

> Peace

> Perspective
> Acceptance
> Other things that may be applicable to you personally, such as:

- Forgiving yourself for actions or statements you regret.
- Improving your anger management.
- Lessening sorrow or sadness due to a loss.

These are incredibly important and meaningful life improvements and lend importance to the value of spirituality.

SPIRITUAL SEEKERS

Since I feel that developing my spiritual side and knowledge has enhanced my own life, I'd like to advocate the idea of having, pondering, developing, and practicing your spiritual beliefs, whatever they may be. If you're interested and open to this journey, let me help you get started. Here's some suggestions on ways to begin:

> Look around you and ask those whom you admire to what they attribute their peace, happiness, or indomitable will to persevere in the face of adversity. You don't have to go far to find examples of people who have achieved remarkable things which they attribute to their spiritual beliefs.

> Find and read stories of others who have endured terrible suffering and even death for similar spiritual beliefs. As Pascal, the French philosopher said, "There are God-sized holes in all of us, and only God can fill these."

> Pay it forward! Mother Teresa once described herself as follows: "I'm just a pencil in the hand of God who is still writing a love letter to man." Wouldn't it be nice if we all helped in the writing of this love letter? Maybe just one small paragraph or even a sentence? The truth is that we can, and it's not even all that hard.

All you have to do is pay it forward and do unto others as you would have them do unto you .... to the extent and frequency your personality allows.

> Consider the many varieties of spiritual beliefs out there; some older and more formal, or more relaxed, like those in *A Course in Miracles*. Most churches, temples, and services welcome visitors so you can determine in person if there might be some comfort and peace to be found in the religious tradition being upheld.

> Do some research on the impact spirituality and religious beliefs can have on someone's life through talking to friends, family, and co-workers if you think they would be open to doing so.

> Use prayer as a means of talking with your higher power, calming down, and releasing any sadness, despair, anxiety, shame, depression, and more. Prayer, after all, is a particular form of reaching out, talking, or even meditation. It can be very helpful as you deal with issues and goals in your life.

Remember we are all different, so use whatever strategy and technique resonates with you.

And as a final thought, consider this: Isn't it just possible that Heaven on earth is knowing how blessed we are and living our lives from that point of view?

CHAPTER 23
STRATEGY – SURROUND YOURSELF WITH FEEL-GOODS

ONE WAY I TRAIN MY mind to keep a focus on thinking and feeling positively is to surround myself with things that make me feel good. I have my feel-goods present in any environment I frequent, whether I'm at home, in the car, in my office, or out socially. Some items bring back fond and/or emotional memories (e.g., of a loved one or vacation), and others represent things of which I am proud or enjoy. For example, my office has several feel-goods on its walls and shelves, such as photos of loved ones and activities I enjoy, or reminders of memorable achievements and events. As for my bedroom I am sure to keep in the front of my closet my favorite shirts and pants I can now wear since I have lost weight. Every time I put them on, they help me feel good.

I literally keep feel-goods with me all day on my person and/or in my pockets! I have 8 in that category as I type this: One is a $1 coin my dad gave me, another is a pocketknife I picked up on a special vacation, and a third is my college ring which I earned due to a lot of hard work. Each time I see, feel, or use my feel-goods during the day, I get a little bit of satisfaction, pride, and a warm fuzzy.

In my opinion, a person just cannot have too many positive memories and thoughts, so why not bring them about by bringing them along as much as possible? They can increase a person's sense of closeness and being loved, while simultaneously increasing feelings of strength, support, and accomplishment. But you have to practice a little to get in the habit of actually seeing the items and concentrating briefly on the positive emotions. If you go unconscious to feel-goods, they lose their positive powers and simply become part of the wallpaper.

WHAT ARE YOUR FEEL-GOODS?

Feel-goods are a personal choice. I enjoy feel-goods that relate to and are helpful in bringing to mind times when I experienced and was enriched by such things as:

> A positive mental attitude
> Gratitude
> Empathy for others
> Something done for me by another, especially a loved one
> Something I did for another
> How I handled a problem, mistake, or some other tricky situation
> An instance when I took charge of my life
> A spiritual experience I had and was enriched by
> A time I handled change well
> When I experienced the richness of delayed gratification
> When I achieved something of importance to me.

If you use the above list as a guide to help in choosing your own feel-goods, the odds are strong that you will be thrilled by your selection. Plus a large body of knowledge indicates that people move in the direction of what they think about and visualize. Having the right feel-goods surrounding you helps in this journey. They will help you keep your thoughts positive, reduce any angst, sadness, upset, or anxiety you feel, and remind you to keep your focus on achieving your dreams and goals. You might even want to set an alarm on your phone or watch to remind you to look at your feel-goods a few times a day, just so you don't forget and zone them out.

One way I remind myself of the importance of positive thinking and feeling good is through the pictures I keep on my computer. In my view, it is worth having a computer just for its slideshow function! You can look up during the day in your office or when you're at home, or even when you're out of town and enjoy seeing pictures of family, friends, vacations, or serene and peaceful shots of pets, nature, etc. Often the first thing I do when getting to a hotel room while traveling is set up my tablet or laptop to run a slide show of some of my favorite pictures. From that point forward in the hotel room, it's like being home.

My wife and I also have at least seven or eight different computers and digital frames around the house on which we run different slideshows 24/7/365 of our favorite pictures of the kids, grandkids, friends, pets, and our vacations.

The simple fact of the matter is this: **The more time you can keep yourself in your feel-good zone, the less time there is for upset, worry, anger, or anxious feelings to creep in and upset your day or week!**

CHAPTER 24

STRATEGY – NOT MY CIRCUS, NOT MY MONKEYS

IF YOU WOULD LIKE PERSPECTIVE with a smile, consider what is happening at the moment and before you get too drawn in, take a few deep breaths and remember this old Polish proverb:

Not my circus, not my monkeys.

What an important point the proverb makes: What upsets another person does not have to upset you! And their problems can be just that ... theirs, not yours! I find it quite valuable and applicable to situations in which other people are running around like chickens with their heads cut off! I am a fan of calm and quiet, so hyperactivity and upset on the part of others can disturb my peace. If I recall the Polish proverb, it generally helps me to chuckle, and see myself separate from the commotion ... and at peace.

This is an incredibly simple but often ignored or overlooked insight to incorporate into how we live our lives! We often tend to take on the emotional state of those with whom we are dealing, and this can be detrimental to our well-being. Their upsets can become ours, and this is not good for us.

You do not have to buy into another person's state of mind. Return to the aforementioned wisdom of the Polish people again and again as you go about your day. The proverb can help you gain perspective, and perspective can aid you in acquiring a deeper understanding of the proverb.

And while you are deciding that certain monkeys are not yours to deal with, be sure to keep them off your back! Not only don't you want to boost them up there yourself, but you should also resist anyone else putting them there as well! You need to delegate effectively and resist reverse delegation whereby the monkey again resides on your back. Most of us have enough to be responsible for, and we do not need to assume responsibility for others' projects or actions. We all have a limit to how many balls we can keep in the air. If you honestly feel that helping is needed, wanted, and appropriate, and if you have the bandwidth available, it is wonderful to offer to help. Otherwise keep doing your own job and let others deal with the crisis of the moment. We all have our own valid crises, perhaps this is simply theirs to deal with.

CHAPTER 25

STRATEGY – IT'S OKAY TO LET THE YOUNG HAVE THEIR YOUTH

LET ME EXPLAIN WHY it's important not to decry growing old through a poem I wrote in November 2008 when I was a mere 65:

ODE TO AGING

Oh my, the joys of growing old
Are so much more than folks had told.
I creak and ache, I pop my knee.
My best friend is my own GP.
The surgeon says it's orthoscopic.
But when that train comes, I won't hop it
'Cause I'll be there ... I'll roll the dice;
To play again I'll sacrifice.
My feet have corns that hurt if I twist
So now I have a podiatrist.
But despite all this my main attentions
Are heart, eyes, mind—and their many henchmen.
I have a small valve that leaks like a sieve,
So another doc is sharpening his shiv.
I've had over 2 billion beats from this heart,
So a valve may be swapped for a small cow part.
My ocular pressure is sky high,
But no damage is done to either eye.
So what if I have early cataracts?
My vision is fine and those are the facts!
If my mind's not racing or gone astray,
It helps me avoid a daily dismay;

But then the neurons start to fade,
Memory goes—where have I laid ...?
My teeth are filled and capped and crowned,
But straightened now—no longer bound.
Soon I'll celebrate and drink a tonic
For with one more crown I'll be bionic.
Some minor problems of the skin,
A bad elbow, an aching shin.
My shoulder joint is bone on bone,
And won't respond to cortisone.
My pressure's high, my cholesterol sucks,
But what the heck if the pills just cost bucks!
Who cares about surgeries on a hand;
I never wanted to be in the band.
It takes only minutes to kill the pain,
But in just a few days it's back again
I've always been a big sugar hound;
But with one look now I've gained a pound.
My hair is thin and getting grey;
It has the feel of fresh crisp hay.
Vitamins and aspirin for the heart,
Omega 3 for those fatty parts.
I truly think the docs believe
I'll take this stuff until I heave.
Pills and capsules, drops and potions;
What would I do without lotions?
It sure makes sense that my pharmacy bill
Is so very high it empties the till.
It may take a village to raise a small child.
And to some folks that may sound pretty wild;
But not to me because I know to my socks:
For me to feel good takes a whole team of doc.s!
While all the above is very much true,
I'm not even a light shade of blue.
Life's way too good to be down or sad,

And these small matters are not so bad.
There are issues and concerns galore,
But there's really nothing to abhor.
These come with our life, and thankfully
The price of poker is almost free.
I know it sounds crazy but despite this stuff
I will be happy 'til I can't even huff.
'Cause the option is plain and not worth discussin.'
There's no point in crying; it doesn't help nothin'!
Yes, things are all great and never better—
The young can have youth—it's just a header.
Life's exquisite—not to be dissed
By thoughts, or fears, or chances missed.
Many things come from the stuff I've done,
But I wouldn't change them—no, not one.
Football, skydiving, and racquet games
Have led to neither wealth nor big fame.
But fun and self cannot be bought,
And I feel lucky to have fought
For a life rich in family and friends;
My gratitude and peace know no ends.

CHAPTER 26
STRATEGY – SURF THOSE WAVES!

IF WE LIVE A LONG LIFE, tough times and pain come to us all. As a result, it behooves us to bear in mind:

> **You can't stop the waves, but you can learn to surf!**

With this attitude and perspective, you understand you can't fight the natural order of things, so you strive to go with the flow when possible. Do your best to see a ray of light during darker times and move forward and enjoy your life despite sorrows and concerns. Live your life and experience joy, freedom, the wind in your hair, and the water beneath your feet despite the obstacles or struggles life sends your way.

To continue with the water metaphor, keep in mind that "ships don't sink because of the water around them; ships sink because of the water that gets INTO them." So don't let what happens around you get inside of you and weigh you down. In this sense, having perspective acts as your waterproofing.

DURING TIMES THAT ARE THE TOUGHEST

Let's be clear, however: There are certainly agonizing, heartbreaking times when even maintaining or relying on principles or strategies does not help. If you hit a problem that is a 15 on the scale of 1-10, all the perspective in the world won't let you sail through it. This might be something like the act of a drunk driver hitting and killing someone in your family, or a friend or family member committing suicide.

In agonizing situations such as these, you just have to marshal all of your resources (that means family, friends, support groups, healthy distractions, and more) and hang onto them until you can find a way through the abyss. Things really ARE that bad! While I may not even know you, please understand that I wish you the very best in any distressing times and situations, and I know that your friends and family do as well. Please let them help.

If appropriate, seek the help of professionals as well: That's why they are there. There's no shame in asking for help, advice, and guidance. I have learned this on my own life's path. Professionals can help guide you through the darkness so you can return to a normal, productive life that might not be possible to achieve otherwise. In my own case, I am virtually certain that without a copious amount of therapy, the application of a fairly light amount of medication, and medical procedures that have only been available for a decade or two, I would not be here to write this book.

It is a sign of great wisdom to realize when you need help, and to get it.

CHAPTER 27
STRATEGY – GET COMFORTABLE WITH DEATH

THIS IS PRETTY MUCH the ultimate change to get comfortable with, isn't it? I consider it as being post-graduate work on getting comfortable with change!

Thinking of one's own death can be a uniquely anxiety-producing and depression-inducing thought process. It is a little hard to get our arms around our mortality, and even harder still to accept it. This may be especially true among those of us who do not experience the strong calming effects of faith.

Having done some work on the subject of mortality over the years, and since I now am over eighty years of age as of this writing, I would like to share a couple of ways that have helped me get more comfortable with my upcoming eventual demise. I find them calming, and they help me put the matter in perspective:

> A certain level of anxiety concerning death is not unusual, and in fact is almost universal. It is very common for people to fear death, the great unknown; I know I completely avoided thinking about it for my first 50 years, but now I'm much more comfortable with it. After all, we don't like change or uncertainty, and no one looks forward to loss. But we can use this anxiety for good in that it motivates us to focus on using our time wisely and in a positive way.

I saw an example of this with a friend of mine who exercises at the same place and same time as I often do. One morning, as I saw him going through his very rigorous exercise routine, I commented to him that it looked like his goal must be to live forever. His comment back to me was, "Who doesn't want to live forever?" For me, that kind of said it all! Clearly this man already realized how much he loved life and that he would die sooner if he didn't do what he could to prolong his life. So there he was, staying fit and healthy!

Also, Norman Vincent Peale, the well-respected minister who popularized the idea of positive thinking, preached of a loving God and afterlife. Yet while he was not afraid of death, he said he did not want to die and had a desire to live as long as possible.

If a man of such strong faith feels that way, why should I feel differently or feel badly about my own desire to prolong my life as much as possible? Who says I shouldn't be interested in living as long as I can, just as Norman Vincent Peale was?

> Learning about death at an early age helps us in dealing with it later in life. Just as it helps in the long run to be exposed to germs early in life in order to build up our immunities, or to see your parents disagree and then resolve things as a way to learn conflict management, there are advantages to learning about death in our early years so that the idea of death will not be so traumatic for us when we consider our own later in life. It is good to grasp that any lack of acceptance will not change the tides of life or alter how the universe works; it will only give us intense stress rather than peace.

My childhood experience with death came through losing pets. When I was about six, I approached my mom one day and proudly announced that my parakeet had learned a new trick of sleeping on its back. That cost our family one brand-new fancy linen napkin and was the cause of a short but meaningful ceremony in an outside flower bed. Also, since my family lived across the street from a high school, it wasn't long before I discovered that to mix outside cats and teenage drivers was not a healthy idea for our feline population. It's why, while growing up, I had many cats!

So I learned about death being in our world in a relatively easy way. In fact, one reason for children to have pets is the acquisition of this knowledge. They come to learn life is not permanent in a less traumatic way than through the death of a parent or sibling. I have to admit, however, that although I did understand at an early age that pets don't live forever, as I said above, I had a much more difficult time facing my own mortality. I mean c'mon ... THAT IS REALLY serious!

> I go on a spiritual retreat annually; and the retreat gives its participants the better part of three days of total silence, allowing each of us to think of the important parts of life that we often do not have the time to consider because of what may otherwise be a busy, hectic life. I have had a number of significant realizations and insights during these annual retreats that I am confident I would not have had otherwise, including some which helped me greatly come to terms with my mortality and consider my eventual fate. It has allowed me to experience insights about death and expand my comfort zone and perspective regarding it.

An example of some of the realizations I've had on this retreat are included in the following letter I composed to my family and which I originally planned to have waiting for them upon my death. I have reread it since creating it and find it to be a gift that keeps on giving! I share significant parts of it here as an example of how dealing with difficult topics can bring a person peace and calm.

Dearest Family,

You may have no idea how much I love you all. It would be hard for me to express and for you to imagine. You have helped to make my life a wonderful experience. Some of the very best times have been when I have felt and truly experienced your love for me and when, in times of need, you have supported and loved me, and most of all, when you have allowed me to do the same for you.

There will come a time when I am no longer with you. I am sad about that because of all the happiness being with you has brought to me over the years. I love you, respect you, honor you, and am amazed and in awe of you.

Do not be sad for me though. I have had a very blessed life! And hopefully, I will always be with you in spirit.

You are each amazing and wonderful in your unique ways. I hope you will always love and support each other in your lives and stay in contact to be a loving, positive part of each other's lives.

I was just walking along the oak-tree-lined path from the Manresa library out past the altar and towards the woods. It is a beautiful, peaceful, and calm walk. It is a little like in "Field of Dreams" when the characters walk into and out of the cornfield. Here, it is the rows of 250+ year old oaks, with more moss on these trees than in the whole of New Orleans. At the end of the straight path through the trees, there is a statue of Jesus on a brick pedestal with his arms extended towards you and with the inscription from Matthew 11:23 on a plaque below: "Come to me, all you who labor and are burdened and I will give you rest." Wow! I think that is what the afterlife may be like, or at least the transition... a beautiful path lined with giant trees leading to an endless forest of green ... the living world behind, and the future world ahead. There will be streams and animals, beautiful colors, and sounds. And there will be eternal peace, joy, and good health. And maybe a coffee bar with apple fritters and brownie sundaes.

Love Always,

Dad/Howard

> I take a practice walk each year at the retreat to assess how comfortable I am walking down the road away from everyone and everything. As I take my practice walk, I think of the type of death I would prefer. I do not dwell on the ways I would not want it to go, since these scenarios are less likely. One reason this kind of practice walk is good is because it desensitizes a person's thoughts around death, in much the same way a person anxious about flying can benefit from getting on and off of standing planes, each time going a little further toward the real experience. Then, when it is time for this person to make an actual flight, it won't be as scary for them. I started doing this type of walk in 2014, and to my relief, but not surprise, this exercise has become easier and easier.

> We can use the thought of death in a positive way every day to encourage ourselves to do important relationship-building and other actions that are meaningful to us. Learn to forgive yourself if you fail and accept yourself if you fall short. If you have trouble doing any of this, remember it takes practice, and try to do better next time.

> It is very important to keep in mind how sad it is when people die full of regrets. Perhaps they didn't strive for what they desired, didn't tell someone they cherished how much they loved them, or didn't try to make amends for or ask forgiveness for something they did which was mean-spirited or hurt others. Feeling this way can be avoided if you intentionally live your life each day as though your life depends on it (which it does) so that you will not find yourself on your deathbed with regrets when it is too late to correct the situation. Think of it as the ultimate in delayed gratification: Doing the work upfront to have a peaceful death. But I would also tell you that it makes your whole life better. And while you may choose not to do this now for whatever reason, it is still good to know it is possible.

> When it's time for us to go, keep in mind that for most of us the pain, suffering, and anxiety that is associated with death in the past will be just that: A thing of the past. We are blessed to live at a time when great advances have been made in pain management. With the advances of modern medicine, much of the suffering most of us fear concerning death can be relieved. If our circumstances warrant these medical and care advances, today we are incredibly fortunate to have them available to us. If the thought of this bothers you, there is no requirement for you to take advantage of them, but I find it comforting to know that the options are there if I choose to use them one day, or if a member of my family were to ask for them on my behalf if I am in a state where I am unable to do so.

> Some of our loved ones and the elderly change their perspective over the years and come to accept or even welcome death. While this can be a troubling thought for some, if you have ever seen someone in pain or worn down by the serious blows of life, you know or may have seen a situation in which death may no longer be so bad for the person involved. The individuals concerned may have had a good, fulfilling life, or even one too filled with loss and sadness to want to continue. Some people therefore "slide into home plate totally used up and fulfilled, with no regrets," while others seek relief from the tormenting mental or physical pain or disability which has built up to an intolerable level. They are tired and ready to go.

When death represents the end of intolerable suffering of any kind, we can come to welcome it.

> Keep in mind on a daily basis this allegory (I discovered it going around the web):

<u>LIFE IS LIKE A TRAIN RIDE</u>

- [Attributed to several authors, so I'm not sure whom to credit]

Life is like a train ride. We get on, we ride, we get off. We get back on and ride some more.

There are accidents and there are delays. At certain stops there are surprises.

Some of these will translate into great moments of joy; some will result in profound sorrow.

When we are born and we first board the train, we meet people whom we think will be with us for the entire journey. Those people are our parents.

Sadly, this is far from the truth. Our parents are with us for as long as we absolutely need them. They too have journeys they must complete.

We live on with the memories of their love, affection, friendship, guidance, and their presence.

There are others who board the train and who eventually become very important to us.

These people are our brothers, sisters, friends, and acquaintances, whom we will learn to love, and cherish.

Some people consider their journey like a jaunty tour. They will just go merrily along.

Others will encounter many upsets, tears, and losses on their journey. Others still will linger on to offer a helping hand to anyone in need.

Some people on the train will leave an everlasting impression when they get off.

Some will get on and get off the train so quickly, they will scarcely leave a sign that they ever traveled along with us or ever crossed our path.

We will sometimes be upset that some passengers, who we love, will choose to sit in another compartment and leave us to travel on our own.

Then again, there's nothing that says we can't seek them out anyway.

Nevertheless, once sought out and found, we may not even be able to sit next to them because that seat will already be taken.

That's okay ...everyone's journey will be filled with hopes, dreams, challenges, setbacks, and goodbyes.

We must strive to make the best of it ... no matter what ... We must constantly strive to understand our travel companions and look for the best in everyone.

Remember that at any moment during our journey, any one of our travel companions can have a weak moment and need our help.

We too may vacillate or hesitate, even stumble; but hopefully we can count on someone being there to be supportive and understanding.

The bigger mystery of our journey is that we don't know when our last stop will come.

Neither do we know when our travel companions will make their last stop. Not even those sitting in the seat next to us.

Personally, I know I'll be sad to make my final stop ... I'm sure of it! My separation from all those friends and acquaintances I made during the train ride will be painful.

Leaving all those I'm close to will be a sad thing.

But then again, I'm certain that one day I'll get to the main station only to meet up with everyone else.

They'll all be carrying their baggage, most of which they didn't have when they first got on this train.

I'll be glad to see them again. I'll also be glad to have contributed to their baggage, and to have enriched their lives, just as much as they will have contributed to my baggage and enriched my life.

We're all on this train ride together.

Above all, we should all strive to make the ride as pleasant and memorable as we can, right up until we each make the final stop and leave the train for the last time...

All aboard and safe journey! BON VOYAGE!!!

THIS REALLY IS A BEAUTIFUL explanation of life and death.

> Another helpful anecdote regarding death is as follows: A sick man turned to his doctor as he was preparing to leave the examination room and said, 'Doctor, I am afraid to die. Tell me what lies on the other side.' Very quietly, the doctor said, 'I don't know. You don't know? You're a Christian man, and don't know what's on the other side?'

The doctor was holding the handle of the door; on the other side came the sound of scratching and whining, and as he opened the door, a dog sprang into the room and leaped on him with an eager show of gladness. Turning to the patient, the doctor said, 'Did you notice my dog? He's never been in this room before. He didn't know what was inside. He knew nothing except that his master was here, and when the door opened, he sprang in without fear. I know little of what is on the other side of death, but I do know one thing: I know my Master is there and that is enough.'

> Finally, reconsider your very notion of the death process. Here's how:

Consider the normal baby, about to be born, floating around in its mother's body. All the baby's needs are being met, so there are no issues, no worries. Then all of a sudden, from the baby's point of view, all hell breaks loose! There is pushing, pressure, possibly something that might be interpreted as pain, bright lights, invasion by strange beings, squeezing, wiping, suctioning, and a slap on the baby's rear end. If he had the ability to think in this way, surely the baby must think he was dying! And yet the process is what we adults call "being born."

Now think about the process that we adults call "death." Is it not possible or even likely that we have that process wrong as well? Why would we be born only to die? Isn't it possible or even likely that what we call dying is just the beginning of another phase of our being? If you obsess about death or operate in complete denial by avoiding the thought of it, there is a cost to you in vitality, attitude, and how you live your life. Why not take a kinder, gentler, more relaxed and accepting view of death? It could very well be that way!

PART IV

SPECIFIC STRATEGIES – WIDEN YOUR HORIZONS

PART IV - OVERVIEW

FOR ME, IT WAS THE question of the chicken or the egg: It was always hard for me to tell which came first, the feeling of complete isolation and loneliness, or the anxiety. I frequently encountered severe anxiety when I traveled for work or other reasons. Simply being away from my friends and family while out of town (isolation) could bring on a large dose of anxious feelings.

Yet when I was anxious, I always felt isolated regardless of where I was. I could be at home, at work, in a store, or away; it simply didn't matter. At those times I also experienced a very narrow focus, mentally and visually. The loneliness also contributed to my having feelings of fear, guilt, sadness, and so forth; it allowed those negative emotions to bubble up.

Whenever I became very anxious, I found it was always quite important that I eliminate the feelings of loneliness and isolation and somehow get additional people into my world. For me, doing this provided an immediate means of feeling better. I found having contact with people was a unique and powerful antidote for my anxiety. They could be complete strangers (e.g., cab drivers, people on the street, or someone sitting next to me on a plane) or friends and family.

To accomplish the elimination of my isolation—a critical part of my healing process— I developed a number of techniques, all by trial and error. If something worked, I did it again—and if it didn't, I threw it out and looked for something else to help me feel better. As always, the idea behind it was to get out of my head and distract myself, not with tricks, but with concrete and positive strategies that would make me feel better.

Let me acknowledge that some of the strategies I'm going to identify below may feel counter-intuitive at first. For example, when you feel your fear, depression, shame or upset increasing, or realize you are in the midst of a full-blown panic attack, reaching out may not be your first thought or inclination. But I believe we can all find occasions when reaching out is possible, and it is at these times that I would encourage you to take such actions to help yourself.

In this section of the book, I offer some specific strategies that helped me reduce or eliminate isolation. I hope you will also find them helpful.

CHAPTER 28
STRATEGY – ELIMINATE ISOLATION

REACH OUT AND TOUCH SOMEONE!

Several decades ago, AT&T used the marketing slogan, "Reach out and touch someone," to promote their phone services. I always liked the concept of making connections with people on a personal basis, so I employed the reach out slogan in my efforts to eliminate the feeling of isolation.

The ways in which we can do this are varied, and I've described a few with examples below. In most of these cases, it was the act of helping someone that made the most difference. The reaching out and touching another human in a way that behooves them can, in turn, also help you with your feelings of isolation.

I like to think of a handshake (or even an elbow bump) as a modified hug, especially when done with feeling. And I believe that sometimes it is almost as good as a hug; it too is a personal contact! When you take the initiative to introduce yourself to someone and shake hands, it's always nice (and in rare instances, almost electric). You actually feel a connection, and that's something which totally changes the mood of the interaction. People's feelings can totally change upon this simple form of touch.

Now let's move on to a result of one of my all-time favorite studies: It showed that a waitperson who touched the customer casually and lightly (and of course, platonically) on the shoulder received anywhere from 7-36% higher tips from their customers than those who had not. This clearly reveals how much of a positive impression the power of touch had on the other people. Choose to give it to someone really in need. Talking to other people about themselves, focusing on them, not yourself, is another fantastic way to calm your mind and eliminate feelings of loneliness; and it can help them feel better as well.

Offering a brief but caring physical touch can do wonders when it comes to eliminating loneliness. Hugs of course, are one of God's great inventions (when used appropriately) to show sincere caring, affection, or support. They are definite "feel-good" passers-on and rarely fail to improve a person's mood. Clinical studies reveal hugs lower blood pressure and can generate relaxation.

I had another example of reaching out and touching someone when I was interacting with a friend who provided me with excellent nutritional and exercise advice. She is a sought-after person who works with TV stations and health facilities and does counseling in her field. By any measure she is a competent and highly functioning individual. During our meeting it soon became clear that I was going to have to do certain things I had not planned on, and the time this work would require would further erode the time I had to work on this book and do some other activities I was already having trouble finding time for. The realization did not cause me to have a panic attack, but I did feel myself become somewhat anxious and uncomfortable. I began to sweat fairly profusely as a result of this new awareness.

Then something interesting happened. Our conversation turned to an area of her life that she was working on and for which I had previously spent some time trying to provide her with some helpful information and counseling. My friend was nice enough to tell me that the help I had given had, in fact, made a difference and aided her in making changes and adopting new practices that made her life better. At this point, my entire outlook changed 180 degrees; I became almost instantly relaxed and felt wonderful. It completely overshadowed the inward, me-centered anxiety! Now I was only thinking of how I had aided her, and I was not even remotely worried about that extra work I was going to have to do. I knew I could do it, and if that was what it was going to take to achieve my goals, well, so be it! Nothing factual had changed, only my attitude and on what I was focusing. I was so happy for her and felt so good that my sweating stopped immediately. A few minutes later when our meeting finished, I realized my face was completely dry.

This focus-on-others strategy is a normal way to reach out and touch people; you engage them as well as yourself. It widens your horizons, stops you from thinking only of yourself, and helps you to return to the real world. The mental and physical activity of engaging in a normal back-and-forth conversation or dialogue can help calm your breathing, keep your mind from racing, and help to stop the isolated feelings you might be experiencing.

I also find talking to cab/or Uber drivers to be calming and enjoyable while I am on the way to the airport and leaving town with a minor dose of Pavlovian anxiety. While not being a particularly chatty person in general, I really like talking to them. These folks generally work long hours, and many are immigrants who think of our country as a haven and a real land of opportunities they don't have in their own countries. I normally try to compliment them on what they are doing with their lives as they strive to reach their dreams and goals. I discovered that when I think I am making them feel better, I feel better as well. Our exchanges often help me realize how very fortunate I am, and how very much I have to be grateful for.

In fact, a *Wall St. Journal* article (November 18, 2014) supported this exact phenomenon. The article referenced a study which found "... commuters who struck up conversations with strangers on trains and buses, and in taxi cabs and waiting rooms, reported greater well-being than others instructed to communicate in their normal way or remain disconnected from fellow travelers." The article further mentioned that the first group enjoyed "a greater sense of belonging and more satisfaction."

To end this section with a personal anecdote: I once had an unusual and powerful experience in Mobile, Alabama. Early in my professional career I was wandering around town at 3-4 a.m. In this place where I was isolated from everyone I knew, I was far too anxious to sleep, so I had left my hotel room to go outside to try and walk the worries away. As I was out, a man approached and asked me for the directions to the bus station. I was able to supply him with this information, and he went on his way. This seemingly inconsequential interaction was like a miracle to me; helping him made me experience an almost instantaneous purging of anxiety, and I was healed, so to speak. I went back to my hotel and fell asleep— instantly!

Helping this man helped me. Period!

To this day, I still look for others whom I can help, especially when I am in times of stress. I feel incredibly better when I am able to do this.

WHEN HELPING OTHERS

There may be two potential concerns on your minds that I'd like to respond to before we move on:

> If finding out this is a strategy raises the question in your mind as to whether doing things with and for others is just a self-serving "feel-good" strategy for keeping anxiety at bay or whether it is a true charitable act, I'd like to share with you my answer to that question: If someone as worthy as Mother Teresa did her good deeds partially to help herself feel better as reported, who am I to question the validity of such actions or to worry about whether they are noble or self-serving? Either way, the helpful actions are not illegal, immoral, or fattening—and they work. Good deeds are done, and everyone on both sides feels better.

> In an environment of the #MeToo movement, some readers might misinterpret the above idea of reaching out and touching someone. Please understand my use of the slogan in no way refers to anything inappropriate and doesn't even necessarily include any physical touching.

PERFORM RANDOM ACTS OF KINDNESS!

Small acts of kindness —e.g. letting someone go in front of you in traffic, sending good thoughts or a small prayer to the person in trouble inside an ambulance as it passes you, or making sure to smile and say hello to your child's teacher or a neighbor—can make you feel more relaxed, grounded, grateful, and at peace.

Take time to engage with a stranger, not just someone you know. It is so easy to take a minute or two to be helpful, friendly, complimentary, and/or supportive to others; and it can make a significant difference to them and to you. So go ahead: Stop and ask someone who is obviously sad or befuddled if you can help them, rather than just continuing to walk by as if you don't care.

Perhaps even join me in anonymously (or not) picking up the meal tab for a service member or first responder, and/or expressing your thanks to them for what they do for us on a daily basis.

Random acts of kindness are extremely powerful.

———◉———

PAY IT FORWARD

This is one of the great concepts of our time, in my opinion, and a sign that there may yet be hope for humankind! The idea is to do something nice for someone else, asking nothing in return except simply that, instead of repaying you, they do something nice for another person under similar circumstances. Instead of the "doing something nice" being contained between two people, a chain reaction is started, and it spreads and spreads. The mental image of this is comforting in itself: there are ripples going outward, as opposed to smaller and tighter concentric circles leading inward. And today, with our improved technology, we can actually verify that doing things for others releases feel-good chemicals, oxytocin and dopamine, in the brain. No wonder we feel better! The feeling can be so pleasurable that you may try to keep or regain them by finding other opportunities to do things for others. As we say in New Orleans, "Let the good times roll!"

If you need to be convinced that paying it forward can be an incredible boost to your mood and attitude, just try it a couple of times. And for more ideas, definitely see the movie "Pay It Forward" if you haven't already.

By the way, while I say above that the pay it forward ideas is one of the great concepts of our time, in fact, it might simply be a rewording of the Golden Rule of "do unto others … " Regardless, it is incredibly powerful and I hope you will give it a try. This idea is another win-win with both sides being benefitted.

———◉———

WHEN WITH OTHERS, SHARE YOURSELF

During any periods of emotional distress and negativity, talk about what's going on with you. Share yourself, be completely open, and talk about the present moment, your history, your feelings—whatever is dominant and present in your mind. This advice differs from advice presented in the "Reach Out and Touch Someone" section in this chapter in that it's from somewhat of a self-interested point of view ... to get help rather than to give someone else help. But doing this is fine if it's needed, as the opening up to another person about your feelings can be therapeutic.

Since we are all adults, I don't look at it as dumping your issues on someone else. The other person is free to indicate, at any point, if they are unable or unwilling to help you at this particular time. Discussing anything that isn't illegal, immoral, or fattening is fair game as far as I am concerned! Also, why rob them of the opportunity to reach out and help you?

You may prefer to select someone to whom you feel close and can comfortably confide in. Talk to them about your feelings in person, or in a phone or video chat. Let out that internal pressure you are feeling. Speaking with loved ones has always been one of the most helpful strategies for me in calming down and feeling less isolated.

And when I have been in a bad place I have spoken to complete strangers, cab drivers, priests, and even friends with whom I had never previously gotten into very personal discussions. I have done this from a point of self-interest, knowing that the sharing and disclosing of my current issue might help me. Some people find it easier to do this with a stranger.

If you're not sure about this strategy, you could choose to test the airing of your concerns sometime with a stranger. As they do not know you and probably will never see you again, set aside any fears and concerns. Just do it in order to see how the sharing and exchange makes you feel. If you find that focusing on yourself with others releases some or all of your pain, anxiety, or sadness, then you have another arrow in your quiver, another tool in your toolbox, for ridding yourself of these unwanted emotions and thoughts. And I truly believe in the innate goodness of people; I think the vast majority are happy to try to help someone in need.

HELP YOURSELF GET BEYOND THE TRAUMATIC LOSS OF A LOVED ONE

Many people manage to get through tragedies full of terrible grief and loss by helping others. I'm sure you have heard many stories of people enduring and surviving unspeakable sorrow by reaching out to help others who may also be in pain. And those who prefer a more anonymous approach to helping others might do something like donating blood or sending money to a charity.

The important thing is, if you are able, to do something nice to avoid being stuck in your grief and loss. Doing something for or with others helps you get out of your head, and it can help your sense of empathy and gratitude.

On a 15th anniversary special of the September 11th terrorist attack, a married couple discussed how they were able to cope with the incomprehensible pain and unspeakable grief they had experienced from losing an adult son on that day. Their decision was to start a foundation in his name that would do good works for others; and on the show, they articulated the insight, "If you want to feel better, go help someone."

I have a wonderful friend who lost her husband to brain cancer. One thing she did was begin to create a special awareness day annually to increase awareness of the disease and promote donations to fight this scourge. She was successful on both a state-wide and national basis, and this helped her healing process.

If this strategy has helped people who experienced such indescribable loss and felt so alone without a beloved member of their family, I think it could help just about anyone.

***

YOU CAN MAKE A DIFFERENCE ALL ON YOUR OWN

Perhaps in the end, we all want to be like the little boy walking down the beach (of life) throwing starfish back into the ocean. An elderly man approaches and challenges the boy saying his actions are useless as there are so many starfish on the beach, that he alone could make no difference. The little boy looks up, smiles, and calmly tells the man, "Well, I made a difference with that one ... and that one, and that one ..." as he continues to throw them back one by one. We can't all cure cancer or merit the Nobel Peace Prize, but we can all certainly be that little boy, doing what we can, where we are, with what we have, to help our fellow travelers. We can make a difference all on our own! And take a minute or two to simply contemplate how the world will change when we do.

Not long ago a friend sent this to me:

> It all matters. That someone turns out the lamp, picks up the windblown wrapper, says hello to the invalid, pays at the unattended lot, listens to the repeated tale, folds the abandoned laundry, plays the game fairly, tells the story honestly, acknowledges help, gives credit, says good night, resists temptation, wipes the counter, waits at the yellow light, makes the bed, tips the maid, remembers the illness, congratulates the victor, accepts the consequences, takes a stand, steps up, offers a hand, goes first, goes last, chooses the small portion, teaches the child, tends to the dying, comforts the grieving, removes the splinter, wipes the tear, directs the lost, touches the lonely, is the whole thing. What is most beautiful is least acknowledged. – Laura McBride, *We Are Called to Rise*

There are millions of good-hearted, empathetic people happy to help others, whether they are friends, family, or complete strangers. Doing things for others, like helping them up if they stumble or listening attentively instead of laughing at their vulnerability, can change a person's whole attitude. When we hear such touching stories, whether it's on the evening news or social media, it helps us be in touch with empathy and can soothe or reduce the negative feelings associated with loneliness, anxiety, guilt, or shame. Such stories can enable change

This is the opposite of circling the wagons around yourself and justifying the way you are or what you have done. Personal contact, and beneficial, thoughtful, caring interaction with others are transformative!

Finally, here is a story of how one person's focusing on another, and demonstrating generosity and caring, can affect the recipient. The piece was originally published in Readers Digest in 1966.

THE BLACK TELEPHONE

When I was a young boy, my father had one of the first telephones in our Seattle neighborhood. The polished case was fastened to the wall, and a shiny receiver hung on the side of the box. For a long time, I was too little to reach the telephone, but I used to listen with fascination when my mother talked to it.

I came to discover that somewhere inside the wonderful device lived an amazing person! Her name was "Information Please," and it seemed there was nothing she did not know. For example, "Information Please" could supply anyone's phone number and the correct time.

My personal experience with this genie-in-a-bottle came one day while my mother was visiting a neighbor. I was amusing myself with the items from the tool bench in the basement, and I whacked my finger with a hammer. The pain was terrible, but there seemed no point in crying because there was no one home to give me any sympathy.

I walked around sucking my throbbing finger until I finally arrived at the stairway. When I climbed up the stairs, I saw it: The telephone!

Quickly, I ran for the footstool in the parlor and dragged it to the landing. Climbing up on the stool, I managed to unhook the receiver and held it to my ear. "Information, please," I said into the mouthpiece located just above my head.

There was click or two before a small clear voice spoke into my ear, "Information."

"I hurt my finger..." I wailed into the phone. The tears came readily enough now that I had an audience.

"Isn't your mother home?" came the question.

"Nobody's home but me," I blubbered.

"Are you bleeding?" the voice asked.

"No," I replied. "I hit my finger with the hammer, and it hurts."

"Can you open the icebox?" she asked.

"Un-hunh."

"Then chip off a little bit of ice and hold it to your finger," said the voice.

After that, I called "Information Please" for everything. When I asked her for help with my geography, she told me where Philadelphia was. She helped me with my math. She even told me that the chipmunk I had caught in the park just the day before would eat fruit and nuts.

Then there was the time Petey, our pet canary, died. I called, "Information Please," and told her the sad story. She listened, and then said things grown-ups say to soothe a child. But I was not consoled. I asked, "Why is it that birds should sing so beautifully and bring joy to all families, only to end up as a heap of feathers on the bottom of a cage?"

She must have sensed my deep concern, for she said quietly, "Wayne [my middle name, which she knew by now], always remember that there are other worlds to sing in."

Somehow, I felt better.

Another day I was on the telephone, and I asked Information Please, "How do I spell fix?" "F-I-X."

All these exchanges took place in a small town in the Pacific Northwest, but when I was nine years old, my family moved across the country to Boston. I missed my Information-please friend very much, and as I grew into my teens, the memories of those childhood conversations never really left me.

Often, in moments of doubt and perplexity, I would recall the serene sense of security I had then. I appreciated now how patient, understanding, and kind the busy operator was to have spent her time on a little boy and his needs.

A few years later on, when I was on my way west to attend college, my plane landed in Seattle. I had about a half-hour or so between planes. Without thinking too much what I was doing, I dialed my hometown operator and said, "Information Please."

Miraculously, the small, clear voice I knew so well said, "Information."

Without having thought about it before, I heard myself saying, "Could you please tell me how to spell 'fix'?"

There was a long pause. Then came the soft-spoken answer. "I guess your finger must have healed by now."

I laughed, "So it's really you. I wonder if you have any idea how much you meant to me during that time?"

"I wonder," she said, "if you know how much your calls meant to me. I never had any children, and I used to look forward to your calls."

I told her how often I had thought of her over the years, and I asked if I could call her again when I came back to visit my sister.

"Please do," she said. "Just ask for Sally."

I called three months later when I was back in Seattle. Aa different voice answered. "Information."

"Is Sally there?"

There was a pause, then, "Are you a friend?" the female operator said.

"Yes, this is Wayne. I'm a very old friend of Sally's."

"I'm sorry to have to tell you this," she said. "Sally had been working part-time for the last few years because she was sick. She died five weeks ago." Then, before I could hang up, she said, "Wait a minute...Did you say your name was Wayne?"

"Yes," I answered.

"Well, Sally left a message for you. She wrote it down in case you called. Let me read it to you."

A moment later she read the words in Sally's note.

"Tell him there are other worlds to sing in. He'll know what I mean."

I thanked her and hung up. I knew what Sally had meant.

....

Never underestimate the impression you may make on others.

Whose life have you touched today?

CHAPTER 29

STRATEGY – THE MILK OF HUMAN KINDNESS!

HAVE A TANKFUL

When you take your car in for maintenance and the service guy tells you that you're a quart low on oil, this can be the sign of a problem with your vehicle. But there are folks out there who are a quart low on the milk of human kindness ... and as it turns out, this too could be a problem, for them as well as others.

In my opinion, empathy is the real milk of human kindness. Being empathetic, helpful, and kind to others, especially those who are less fortunate or who are disadvantaged by birth or other circumstances, is one of our best, highest, and finest human characteristics. Getting more of this and nurturing it can bring us happiness and satisfaction.

Empathy for others is outward-focused and helps us keep the focus of our attention off ourselves and on to others, thereby widening our horizons. It helps reduce our anger and general negative emotions and increase our positive ones.

Gratitude reduces negative emotions too, in particular feelings of sadness, regret, and guilt. It is different than empathy because it is somewhat inward-focused and personal, but empathy and gratitude are closely related. Both are sensitivity issues, and I could argue that they normally go in tandem: It seems to me that a person lacking in empathy would likely be lacking in gratitude as well. Seeing the issues and difficulties that others must deal with can help put our own problems in perspective and help us achieve gratitude for our own gifts. On the other hand, if you have no gratitude for your own blessings, you would be less likely to be empathetic towards others.

DON'T ASSUME

Sometimes it is hard not to negatively judge people lacking empathy for others, but we have to know their life story before this attitude has a chance of being justified. Perhaps, for example, they were abused or victimized as a child or adult; maybe they are a person who experienced extreme tragedy in their lives, such as losing loved family members in a natural disaster; maybe they endured extreme poverty for much of their lives; or perhaps they were given up by their parents and never experienced a stable home life.

Since we very rarely know others at this level, perhaps it's best if we place the default setting as to our thoughts about them on feeling sorry for such individuals. If someone lacks empathy or compassion for other individuals, it is difficult to imagine that they can express love or experience gratitude or happiness in our own lives.

MAKING EMPATHY MORE A NATURAL PART OF YOU

If you are not naturally an empathetic person, I have the following suggestions as to how you can begin trying to develop this trait:

> Practice mentally putting yourself in the troubling situations you see around you. Think of how you would feel in those same circumstances, and ask yourself, "What if that were me?" This could include situations where you see people being treated rudely or taken advantage of. We all want to be nurtured, cared for, appreciated, and accepted; and there is no better way to receive this than to understand that other people want and deserve this as well, and to offer it to others.

> Interact with different people (those who hold different beliefs, ethnicities, income, or education levels, for example) to build a base from which you can see the value of empathy. You might take a job or volunteer at a non-profit organization so that you can see, interact with, and help others who might be victims of a

disability or illness. As the Golden Rule says (something which is valued and expressed similarly in many different religions), "Do unto others as you would have them do unto you." In addition to simply thinking empathetically, it is good to act that way as well. After all, it is your actions that others see. The world generally does not know your thoughts.

<hr>

EMPATHETIC ASSERTIVENESS, THE FACETS OF A NUANCED LIFE

"Life is short; don't waste yours by living someone else's. Have the courage to follow your heart and intuition." - Steve Jobs

One could make an argument that empathy (the ability to understand and share another's feelings) and assertiveness (confidently standing up for your beliefs) lie at opposite ends of spectrum. And while both are good in their own way, at times too much of either can be unproductive or unsociable.

You do not have to look far to begin listing the virtues of empathy: being able to forgive others, respecting and considering the opinions and feelings of others, and showing emotional intelligence.

Yet it is also appropriate to be assertive at times. Who else will look out for you if you do not? It gets pretty old and frustrating to never stand up for yourself or exercise your hard-earned personal confidence, as well as your communication and conflict resolution skills.

My personal goal is to blend the two into what I call empathetic assertiveness. For me, this is a situation-based way of interacting with others that generally leans towards empathy...unless I feel that is no longer justified.

You might be wondering, "Where do I draw the line?" My response is: Simply and honestly do your best to balance the two. There will be times when you nail it and others when you don't. Learn from them both and continue to refine and hone these skills. Life will present you with an almost limitless number and variety of circumstances with which to practice each skill set.

It is definitely a lifelong journey to improve yourself and/or your skills (think asymptotic - you can get better and better but never reach perfection); and all you can hope to do is to improve your batting average. Sometimes you will get a walk, a single, a double, a triple, or even a home run—but you'll have strikeouts as well.

Learn to love the game of life and the journey!

CHAPTER 30
STRATEGY – APOLOGIZE AND FORGIVE

MIRACLES (YES, MIRACLES!) can come from our apologies and forgiveness. In fact, apologies are the other side of the coin from forgiveness. You forgive others for what you or they perceive they have done to you; and you apologize for what you or they feel you have done to them.

Giving a sincere apology can be a big step in getting past any guilt, shame, or regret you may be experiencing in your life. The job of the offender is to apologize; the job of the offended party is to forgive.

Without offering someone an apology for something that you believe you have done wrong, or which hurt another, you perpetuate negative feelings such as anger, sadness, or fear. Your mind can spin out of control and go crazy with attempts to justify what was done, making yourself right while enumerating why the other person is wrong, making plans for revenge, and so on. All of this rationalizing does little good.

In fact, many knowledgeable people believe forgiveness does more for the person doing the forgiving than for the other person. It keeps us from being eaten up with anger, stress, and other negative emotions, all of which tend to make us feel isolated. Consider this statement from *A Course in Miracles*:

> **FORGIVENESS OFFERS EVERYTHING I WANT.**

Apologizing does the same! How so? Both types of statements feel good and ultimately are freeing. Neither is easy for anyone in all circumstances—but it diminishes us and narrows our lives when we cannot apologize or forgive.

Offering apologies and forgiveness is both cleansing and freeing, with you being the primary beneficiary! Doing so reduces your stress levels and diminishes your negative feelings and emotions. You end up with a brighter outlook on the day and in your life.

RECOGNIZING THE POWER OF FORGIVENESS

An excellent article in the *Wall Street Journal* on March 20, 2016, was, "The Healing Power of Forgiveness" by Diane Cole. Some of her thoughts are noted below:

> In the absence of forgiveness, an offense that was committed against us ... can replay in our minds and lead to isolation and loneliness ... continuing anger or remorse, and this is often a recipe for bitterness and bad health.

> Not forgiving is tantamount to suffocating yourself emotionally, according to Professor Amit Sood at the Mayo Clinic. The effects of bottled-up anger and resentment can range from anxiety and depression to higher blood pressure and an increased risk of heart attack. Forgiveness, by contrast, allows one to focus on more positive thoughts and relationships, he says, and it frees up the real estate in your brain which was otherwise taken up by your negative thinking.

> If the other party is not willing to do his share in the forgiving (or apologizing) process, you can still let go of your negative feelings, accept the facts of what happened, and move on. As Professor Sood points out, forgiveness is not saying the other person was right ... it is not justifying or condoning, it is simply acknowledging that you have decided to forgo anger and resentment.

> Dr. Janis A. Spring, a clinical psychologist in Westport, Conn adds that you need to be prepared for rejection if you seek forgiveness. It will not always be granted, but it is especially worth the effort as one or both of the parties begin to age. It hurts to take misunderstandings to the grave, and no one profits from that.

I have had several experiences in my life that left me feeling mistreated or unjustly dealt with. I don't hold myself out as a person who forgives quickly or easily in circumstances that really matter to me, but I am generally happier to apologize or forgive and bear no grudges. The difference this has made in my life has been monumental! It is an unpleasant and isolating way to live when consumed with the anger, justification, guilt, and frustration associated with being unforgiven, or being unwilling to apologize. What I've noticed is that I have certain strategies that generally work well for me and which, over time, I do pretty much automatically.

For comments or actions which I find upsetting, or which bring me to anger:

> First, I usually write them down. This is an immense help to me in quieting my mind, stopping endless repetition, and rehashing.

> Next, I try to employ perspective by putting myself in the other person's shoes, thinking of their trials and burdens, while also remembering my own situation. I also evaluate whether the matter is even worth being bothered about; and seeing if I can or should just let it go.

> I engage in a little physical exercise. This always helps to clear out any negative emotions.

These steps are not complex or difficult, but they do help me in getting through almost all potential problems. They have the added advantage of being completely within my control.

As for the time I need to forgive: It generally takes between 10 seconds and 2-3 days for me to get past the issue. If it goes beyond that I know I have to engage with the other party.

In one instance I recall well, I was still steamed after the normal 2-3 day cooling off period. I felt I had been slighted and excluded from an event I thought I should have been invited to. I used my notes to write down and fire off what I thought was an assertive but fair complaint to the other person, only to have her fire back an assertive but equally fair rebuttal! As is common in such circumstances, I was unaware of certain facts, and once I had been made aware of her perspective on the matter, the end result was that we became much better friends with greatly increased respect for each other.

IF PRIDE STANDS IN THE WAY OF APOLOGIZING

It can be a real hurdle for some of us to apologize, but the good news is that the payoff is a release of good feelings; and it can actually increase your self-esteem. Offering an apology at times is a hurdle you can and should cross over, so don't let pride or ego stand in your way or be an obstacle. Give it a try!

Be realistic: We all make mistakes and cleaning them up appropriately can be a big step in a positive direction. Once you start doing so, you should find it easier to apologize as time passes because you will have learned:

> You are not your mistakes, and your apologies make you a bigger and better person!

There is nothing demeaning or weak about making an appropriate, called-for apology. How do you know when you should apologize to another? As a rule of thumb, ask yourself, "Would I expect an apology from the other person if our roles were reversed?" If your answer is yes, then get busy and apologize! It is good for the soul as well as the relationship, whatever it might be.

> When anxiety holds you back from an apology:

Sometimes we don't apologize to one another because we're anxious or nervous about doing so. Your anxiety may be related to something you did, failed to do, said, or failed to say. For instance, you may not want to apologize and be reminded of the transgression, or you could be uncomfortable being around someone when you know you owe that person an apology.

If and when this is the case, do your best to rectify it. I have found that doing so frees me from negative thoughts and a generally non-productive mindset. I feel better, I feel a sense of honesty and integrity, and the world seems brighter.

Let me help you with the "how" of it all.

HOW TO APOLOGIZE

An apology should be both sincere and complete. If you are not sincere, you demean yourself. It is better not to give a halfhearted apology; wait until you can be really sincere. In terms of "complete," I mean that you should cover all of the details of the actual transgression. For example, you might say "I'm sorry that I went behind your back and asked the boss to put me in charge of this project without discussing it with you first." When you are vague, the person receiving the apology may be unclear as to what you are actually sorry for, and this detracts from the healing power of the apology. It can even make the situation worse.

Be sure to limit the apology to the specific situation or transgression. I don't recommend falling all over yourself to get others to forgive you just because the other person may be upset about things. If you do not feel an apology is warranted, giving one can be demeaning. Also, if you apologize for simply everything that's gone on between the two of you from day one, it is too broad; and you diminish your integrity and self-worth.

But when an apology is appropriate to the situation or behavior at hand, do it...the sooner, the better!

CHAPTER 31
STRATEGY – CONTROL YOUR LIFE

WHO RUNS YOUR LIFE?

It is possible to write a whole book on this question, but let's just look at the big picture for a minute. If you do not run your own life and if you are not in charge, then who is?

Let's set the stage before we answer the question. Almost all of us have the following that we deal with:

> One or more bosses at work (for many years, I had 5 simultaneously!)
> A spouse or two (hopefully one at a time) or a significant other
> Children, parents, siblings, and other family members
> Friends
> Upcoming social, spiritual, or community obligations we have accepted
> Many additional time commitments e.g., sleep, medical, fitness
> Personal time, just for ourselves.

Because of these obligations and responsibilities, we may feel like we are not totally in charge of our lives. And some of us may mutter, with a degree of embarrassment, "It's my _________________ (fill in the blank with: mother/father/sister/boss/kids, etc.) who runs my life." We often answer the question this way since that's to whom or what we commit our time and prioritize our focus and tasks.

NOW, WHO DO YOU WANT TO RUN YOUR LIFE?

Read the extremes of the following two possibilities for a minute, and consider which you really want:

1. First, think about what happens if you surrender control over your life and take no responsibility for any part of it. You are likely to be whipsawed by others' demands on you. You may feel like a pawn in the chess game of life, a pinball launched by others, or a piñata surrounded by masses of folks with bats.

If you surrender to everyone else's preferences and try to satisfy all their requests or demands on your time, it is virtually impossible to ever find peace or be a happy camper. You are squandering your potential happiness on the whims of chance and those with agendas different from your own, and the outcome is not likely to be satisfying or pretty. Yes, you get to blame others for your problems (they did it to me!) and avoid taking responsibility for your life and circumstances—but this does not bring peace or satisfaction.

2. At the other extreme, you have total freedom to do as you like. While your happiness is in no way guaranteed, at least in this instance you definitely have the possibility of achieving it. Having total control over your life entails taking responsibility for what happens, which may be a bitter pill to swallow at times. But it is a very reasonable price to pay for what you can get!

My own opinion on the subject is:

> **The more we take responsibility for and control of our own lives and the more we are in charge, the higher the probability is for us to find happiness!**

I submit that, to be content, proud, and fulfilled, you need to be the primary person responsible for, and in charge of, running your life—in all major respects. This includes being responsible for your own mistakes and screwups...but so what? In the first place, it is only fair and right; and in the second place, others undoubtedly will blame you for those mistakes no matter what, so you might as well own up to them. This not only feels better (it's hard to feel really good when you know you are lying), but it is also a positive lifestyle in which you can feel good about your efforts and even small successes rather than living in the negative mindset of look-what-they-have-done-to-me-now! Also, living life this way gives you the important platform from which to require that others take responsibility for the consequences of their own actions!

SHOULD IT BE A "YES" OR A "NO?"

When you take on a commitment or when someone asks you to take on an additional responsibility, do it knowingly and only after giving it reasoned thought as to the potential consequences. This is why others caution us to take a few deep breaths or a few days to think about all the ramifications before accepting new commitments. As a result of learning to do just this, I ultimately chose to limit my activities somewhat throughout my life to allow for concentration on the things that mattered most to me. As for your own goal here, it is to make conscious decisions about your life and be in charge of and responsible for them.

If you feel you are out of control and are not running your own life to a sufficient degree, pick one area of your life, establish a beachhead there, and progress from that point. Or if you are like most folks who have at least some degree of autonomy in terms of their own lives, evaluate the different options you have for expanding your control. For example, if you are doing well in your profession but not well in your personal life, you might decide to cut back a little on some of your work hours to devote more time to your important personal relationships.

At this point I feel compelled to address the almost universal reaction we have to want to say yes when asked to take on a task. We want to satisfy the voice in our heads that tells us "You should," etc. But, please don't lose sight of the big picture. Only you can set your long-term priorities and only you know what brings you satisfaction. Remember that if you end up saying yes to everything, you can't do your best work or build the best relationships when seething or frustrated inside because you now feel like you are doing too much or being taken advantage of. No one can do it all and each of us has his limits; therefore it stands to reason that a no is appropriate at times.

Be aware that while saying no might seem very hard before you actually try it, once you do it you will end up being blown away with how wonderful it feels and how much easier saying no gets over time! Trust me, as a recovering perfectionist and pleaser, I am speaking from experience.

Also, I can tell you that you will get some odd looks or unusual reactions from time to time when you give an unexpected answer. But only you know the true consequences if you say yes, and a no can be the correct response. In addition I believe that if you continue to do quality work, you will earn respect from others even with reasoned no's.

Naturally, you can't let the pendulum swing too far the other way and always say no, live a purely hedonistic life, and attend only to your own whims and desires. That certainly is not a recipe for a happy, fulfilled life! Learn to choose wisely, enjoy the victories, and correct, if appropriate, for any problems you may cause. The upside of taking responsibility is unlimited and can be incredibly life-affirming; the downside is really negligible, and you get to be the one who runs your life! Like empathetic assertiveness, in the end this is a matter of balancing extremes.

MINDFULLY CREATE YOUR DESTINY

Certainly, we all adopt ideas from others and adapt our ways accordingly—but hopefully only when we truly agree with them or feel it's the best course for us. If you are doing this, you are creating your own destiny!

Still, some compromise is often advisable. The opinions or desires of those whom we love, live with, or work with, matter, and often matter very much to us. Just as true is the fact that all of our overlapping obligations may, from time to time, make us feel like just a leaf in the stream of life being forced to go where the current leads.

But no matter how many people and constraints you have to deal with, it is very important that you do so willfully and intentionally. Make the trade-offs and take responsibility for them. It is critical to feel you retain control to a sufficient degree to satisfy your own needs. It is not possible for me to be specific here as everyone is different and their situations are unique, but you will know how you are doing in this area by how you feel (e.g., Am I content or anxious, somewhat sad, stressed, etc.?). This relates to the real possibility of creating the job you want at work as well as achieving the life you want.

Being willful and intentional about your life is not easy; continuing work is needed to achieve balance, and sometimes it feels like that balance is very short-lived. Almost certainly, you will make mistakes from time to time and have the opportunity to learn from them. Also you should learn to make appropriate apologies, as well as mitigate and make up for any damage you may do. Finally, your efforts to be yourself and run your own life will not meet with acceptance in every situation, so it's pretty much guaranteed you will end up having other choices to consider and more decisions to make!

———⟶ ◉ ⟵———

BE OKAY WITH THE CONSEQUENCES

Accept that you cannot please everyone in all situations. That is normal; but still make your decisions and be responsible for them. And because you've made them after consideration, be willing to accept the consequences—no matter what they may be—and do your level best to be happy.

Sometimes the options before you feel limited and certain decisions seem unavoidable, even when they are not pleasant ones. For instance, you may have to give up a short-term goal temporarily (e.g. having more time off) in order to achieve a higher or greater long-term goal (financial security and career success). Be prepared for that. Knowingly make the important decisions in your life (not all decisions <u>are</u> important), and be prepared for some disagreement, argument, upset, and/or pushback from time to time from those around you. This too is unavoidable if you really want to control your life. If you are like I used to be (Mr. Please Everyone), this can be a very uncomfortable thought, but it is just a fact of life; and the alternative is to surrender your life and happiness to others' control.

While controlling and living your own life is a skill very few of us fully master, it is certainly a productive one to pursue our entire lives. If we take responsibility and handle the matters before us with honesty, fairness, and dignity for all parties, we are well along our way to a happy life.

CHAPTER 32
STRATEGY – BE YOU

"BE YOURSELF; EVERYONE else is already taken!" - Oscar Wilde

"Be who God created you to be and you will set the world on fire" - St. Catherine of Siena

Soooo ... be yourself! This sounds easy in one sense, but it can be quite the challenge. Many people avoid thinking about who they actually are because it is not a pleasing image for them, or it brings up conflicts with other goals. For example, this might be tough for people who have a poor self-image or don't especially like the person they think they really are; who are trying to fit in; who are trying to go along just to get along; or who might be attempting to get that promotion at work, perhaps by being overly solicitous or going along with questionable demands. They have become accustomed to playing a part, in essence, to avoid showing their true self to others.

The truth is that, if you try to get in touch with how magnificent you really are, you can begin to improve your self-image and begin to love yourself. And if, as you are getting in touch with yourself, you realize you need some tweaking and want to change certain things about yourself, you can get busy and do that too!

Do not sublimate or sell out your true self to a greater degree than is acceptable to you in the spirit of compromise and love. Each person's level of acceptance is different, but the body and mind have ways of telling you if you have gone too far. We call some of the more pronounced of these ways: anxiety, depression, panic attacks, nightmares, and so on. All these discomforts are horrible to experience; but more importantly, they can act as a warning system for your mind and body that you may be sublimating yourself too much.

As Dr. Ellen Vora said in her book *The Anatomy of Anxiety:*

> **"Anxiety is the 'check-engine' light of life."**

THE KEY TO CONSISTENCY

Being yourself involves developing consistency among the things you say, think, and do. This may sound rather simple, but only if you have not tried it! It is not at all easy at first—but ultimately it is quite freeing.

If you do not show the real you, how can you ever be loved for who you really are? If you feel you need to hide certain aspects of yourself, your life, or lie to be loved, you are not letting anyone see the real you. Be honest with others. Why? How about this great reason:

> Your real self will come out at times, one way or another. You cannot stuff away your true feelings without having them affect your actions, your feelings, and your statements in some way. This is similar to the reactions of a water balloon or a drop of mercury: When you push it in one place, it pokes out in another. Similarly, your mind and your real beliefs are very tough to fool, and often signals like fear or anxiety are there because your mind senses conflict.

HAVE FUN WITH IT

It is perfectly okay to be different and to be yourself, so have some fun with it! Do things others would not do, simply because it's fun, liberating, and confidence-building to be a little different from the rest of the pack.

Besides, at the end of the day, few things are that important. Ask yourself, "How bad is it really? Who really cares?" If you get the right answers back, go for it.

Let your little inner imp or devil out sometimes! I'm not suggesting anything really bad, as in something immoral or illegal; and certainly, don't lie or choose to deliberately hurt someone else. But to help get you started doing things that you might not do otherwise, here are some examples of things I have done that still make me smile although I was somewhat reluctant to do at first:

> Be in pictures with my family members instead of being the one excluded because I was the one always taking the picture. (I actually wanted to be in those shots! So, I spoke up and changed things.)

> Share with friends who, after an operation, were having emotional issues. (I never used to be transparent about my own emotional or mental health difficulties.)

> Join a couple of exercise classes attended only by the other sex. Most men shy away from classes like this, or never continue to attend them after trying once or twice. But I found it quite fun, and I've added many friends...including several who definitely can kick my butt.

> Attended a show with my older brother, Henry, also a computer and gadget enthusiast. We wanted to go to the Consumer Electronics Show in Las Vegas, but there was one slight problem with our attendance: It was open only to people in that industry, and technically my brother and I did not qualify. Undaunted by that minor little hurdle, my brother and I got creative. Since he had worked in the computer industry for years prior to this and we also had both helped others with computer issues, we ordered up business cards with the name, H & H Computer Consulting Service. I was prepared to set up a corresponding dummy corporation, but it turned out that submitting the business card was all that was required. So, for $30, we were good to go and had a terrific time. Our partaking in this event is a good example of "Who cares; did it hurt anyone; and is it immoral, illegal, or fattening?" It is up to each of us to choose how we act or react, and how far we are willing to push the boundaries; but let's be

honest, we all jay-walk, right? And most people drive above the speed limit at times. Similarly, there are an almost infinite number of situations in which the decision is simply a matter of degree.

Now that I have mentioned some specific activities above that I have found helpful, the idea is for you to do something you find enjoyable and pleasing but might not necessarily do ordinarily.

› ENJOY WHAT YOU CONSIDER LIFE'S SMALL PLEASURES

MAKE ROOM IN YOUR SCHEDULE for what you find to be especially enjoyable activities, from drinking a relaxing cup of coffee, to visiting with a friend, going to see a movie, or watching a TV show. Just try to take a little time daily to relax in the ways that work for you. Be your unique self!

CHAPTER 33
STRATEGY – BRING IN THE PETS!

WHEN I WAS FRUSTRATED and upset in my childhood, I found solace in hugging my cat. Sure enough, pets became an indispensable part of my life, and I have never been without a cat for any appreciable time, nor would I want to be. I have always told my wife that if she ever needs to put me in "a home," she just needs to be sure it is one that allows cats!

In college, I listened to my comparative religion professor say that if there were no dogs in heaven, he did not want to go! It's a sentiment with which I totally identify.

PETS PROVIDE!

Life is so comfortable and relaxing when your cat purrs or your dog wags his tail for you and at you! Having a pet provides people with scientifically proven benefits, including:

> Reducing blood pressure

> Helping a person to relax

> Improving a person's mood through interactions with petting, talking to, or playing with a pet.

Pets can be real substitutes for having people in your life, and an improvement in some cases! They definitely help reduce or eliminate feelings of isolation and loneliness.

The difference between coming home to a pet or to an empty apartment or home is the difference between night and day—just ask any pet owner!

It is no surprise that people bring comfort or therapy animals into hospitals and nursing homes to lift patients' spirits and wellbeing, and that people who suffer from PTSD or other forms of anxiety, depression, etc. are allowed to bring their service animals on an airplane.

Along with all this, pets provide the healing powers of touch to those of us who stroke and cuddle them. There's a resulting release of helpful hormones such as oxytocin, and we end up feeling better, in much the same way that people who exercise experience the runner's high. These hormones aid us in relaxing and getting over the stresses of daily life.

Many of us value our pets so much, we consider them members of our family and treat them accordingly. We give them treats and food that rivals our own; paying for pet spas as well as vet care equivalent to the best human health care; and perhaps bury our departed, beloved pets in pet cemeteries or have them cremated, ultimately holding onto, or scattering the ashes, just as we do with those of our human loved ones.

MENTAL UPSIDES

Aside from the advantages noted above, pets have other beneficial impacts on our mental health. They can provide a source of unconditional love and acceptance—and we can never have too much of these. This is especially true for people neglected or abused in some way in their childhoods by the adults who were supposed to love, care for, and protect them.

Studies show that good things come when we care for others. This is true even if the others are small furry souls! When we interact with our pets, it is through at least four of our five senses, as well as our minds and emotions. This is socialization and reaching out and touching someone. All this affects us positively on a primal level and focuses the mind on an experience of relaxation, happiness, and affection. Little wonder that it works so well!

To interact with a pet most people choose to own a pet. However, news articles are replete with the beneficial effects that occur when pets are introduced, sometimes on a limited basis, into the lives of neighbors, retirement living communities, and even prisons.

———⬥———

PETS COMES IN ALL SIZES, SHAPES, AND VARIETIES

I acknowledge that I am partial to cats! But I have also had hamsters, parakeets, a turtle, flying squirrels, and a baby raccoon. Naturally, I know a lot of people who love dogs like I love cats, and I have also had several sweet dogs; they are wonderful too. It is not their fault that they were not born cats. My two older sons and a great nephew have each had pythons, but I disavow all affiliation with those! I also have a friend who dearly longs for a llama as a pet. Well ... okay.

PART V

SPECIFIC STRATEGIES – TAKE ACTION

PART V - OVERVIEW

ON MANY SUNDAYS IN my past, I attended NFL games; but time after time I was not able to remotely enjoy myself due to my excessive anxiety. I assure you I would have gladly exchanged these times and my money for the peace, relaxation, and productivity that comes with a quiet, calm mind.

Guess what! I did something about it. I kept looking and exploring until I found strategies and LOU's that helped me get to a place where I could enjoy myself at these football games and also be more content and calmer throughout the day. There simply is no reasonable price you shouldn't be willing to pay for good mental health and the ability to find your way through life and relationships while performing at an approximation of your highest ability level.

Since I'm referring to the NFL in the above example, and those games usually air with tons of beer commercials, I would like to quote something that a beer commercial used to say: "Stay thirsty, my friend!"

> **Stay thirsty for improvement in your life and for deeper, richer experiences.**

Be willing to look at the areas in your life that aren't working for you as you would like, and don't let pain, despair, misery, or inertia hold you back. Explore, research, and discover! And if necessary, change your attitudes and thought processes to have a happier, more productive life with better relationships, more thrills.

Take action; go for it!

CHAPTER 34

STRATEGY – THE BEST THINGS IN LIFE AREN'T ALWAYS FREE

THE ACTIVITIES, EXPLORATIONS, and knowledge I'm recommending throughout this book may, at times, require you to expend quite a bit of effort. For example, you may need to do extra work to earn the money that's necessary to attend therapy sessions (the subject of the next chapter), or you might research to see if you can find free or sliding-scale pricing options. Yet I believe if you pursue something that brings you increased mental, physical, and/or emotional well-being, you will be glad you did, even if it has a financial cost associated with it.

If you desire to take on therapy or any activity that brings you happiness, but in a way that doesn't upset your budget, consider this: Using therapy as our example yet again, a person might see their therapist once a week for approximately 50 minutes. Now compare the cost of therapy to the dollar amount many of us spend multiple times a week on other activities such as drinking, smoking, gambling, fishing, hunting, boating, skiing, visiting the salon for a manicure, or a massage, and so on. My recommendation is to evaluate the actual costs of these different engagements, then choose to pursue what you believe will bring you the most long-term happiness. In other words:

> **Intentionally direct your dollars in the most fulfilling direction!**

If by engaging in a certain activity you come to find your inner peace and happiness, isn't that the most incredible gift, pleasure, and accomplishment? The financial price tag undoubtedly is well worth it!

CHAPTER 35
STRATEGY – MAXIMIZE PROGRESS WITH THERAPY

"You can learn better, faster, and at lower 'cost' than simply to rely on [your own] experience." - Heinrich Heine, German poet, and critic (1797-1856)

FOR THE MOST PART, the strategies in this book are things you can do on your own—you can go a long way toward healing yourself! There is much you can do for you.

But, if your life is seriously affected by anxiety or any other mental or emotional issue, one of the first options to consider is to seek counsel from a mental health professional. An independent, seasoned healthcare professional can supercharge your improvement and recovery. And if you do so in conjunction with some of the strategies and LOU's offered in this book, the progress you make can be even faster. Even if you might be able to improve your life over time on your on, you can multiply your efforts, go further, greatly increase your chances of success, and get to an even better life faster if you seek help from an understanding, qualified professional.

Therapy can prove effective and beneficial for these reasons (among others):

> Without someone to help us, it is virtually impossible to sift out all of our bias, projection, prejudgments, self-justifications, ego, stubbornness, and so forth. Simply put, living as you do inside of your mind and body prevents you from seeing things as accurately and clearly as a trained professional who has objectivity along with experience and training in the area.

> As German poet and critic Heinrich Heine once said, "Experience is a good school, but the fees are high." It often takes more time, and lots of struggle, pain, and temporary defeats, if you move on the path toward victory while living as if you are an island.

> It's tough, at best, to get the full depth, breadth, and range of improvement all on your own; trying to do it all by yourself is infinitely more difficult. You may believe you see yourself clearly, objectively, and independently (many of us think that), but it is not an easy thing to actually do. It just isn't something the mind does well at all.

> Therapy provides a safe place to explore private and painful episodes in your past and uncomfortable situations or feelings. You can openly discuss and share problem areas in your life and a variety of strategies to deal with them that you may not have considered in previous times. Having the opportunity to verbalize fully in a non-judgmental environment with an educated professional in the areas of concern to you can lead to incredible positive changes on your part.

> You can slow down the world, allowing you to focus and concentrate on specific problems and events, while simultaneously considering the big picture. A healthcare professional who helps you see the big picture more clearly can help you realize you have much more to be hopeful about and grateful for than you might normally realize on your own.

> Therapy can aid you in challenging some of your assumptions. A therapist can help you see new alternatives and rethink whether your current views are clear, realistic, and productive. For instance, assumptions such as, "I will get better with age," or "I might be able to handle my issues on your own, or with the help of a significant other," may be incorrect or inaccurate. Life offers no

guarantees, and in many cases, you could simply be wrong—thereby jeopardizing your health and/or happiness.

> Therapy can help you break the hold that painful or traumatic events or conditions may have had on you, and the adverse effects they may have produced in your life. For example, a therapist might help you think and reframe versus simply reacting to troubling situations or triggers. There's a period of time that always exists between a stimulus and our response, and therapy combined with practice can greatly help expand that time period and provide you with infinitely more beneficial and productive options than the knee-jerk reactions you may have been following. This applies to thoughts as well as actions.

> A therapist can give you powerful new tools to use in daily life. He or she can provide you with important opportunities to:

- Spot internal contradictions, double standards, inner conflicts, blind spots, unfairness, unproductive thought or action patterns.
- Work through your issues,
- Alter how you handle situations,
- Decide on courses of action,

- Road test your ideas and changes with an independent, knowledgeable professional,
- Reach life-changing conclusions, and an almost unlimited list of other potentially troublesome topics and thoughts.

> A therapist can help you see what is missing or not working in your life or relationships and encourage you to go out and find or correct this.

> Therapy can help you work toward the goal of having comfort, calm, relaxation, happiness, and fun, while shedding or lessening fear, guilt, regret, anxiety, shame, bitterness, and panic. Therapy can help you better understand, accept, and deal with your

feelings, and change habits or thought patterns you feel are appropriate to change.

> The process can increase your productivity. You can become more effective as you take your new skills into the world without such burdens as depression, shame or embarrassment, anxiety, etc. holding you back.

> You can reduce the stress you feel and experience more relaxation.

> You can increase your sense of well-being.

> Therapy can help you realize that while you are unique, you are definitely <u>not alone</u> with your issues.

STAY WITH IT

These days, if you're addicted to drugs, alcohol, etc. there is generally a 12-step program available to help. The advice and best practices followed by those who have succeeded are to attend meetings and continue to deal with the addictions and the emotional issues related thereto for the rest of their lives.

Emotional issues are, in a sense, addictions as well—maybe not technically, but they do involve habitual thinking and/or acting in potentially harmful and definitely suboptimal ways. In the case of emotional issues, the way to deal with them is also to keep doing the work. I don't know that anyone ever reaches their ultimate potential for dealing with issues and emotional situations, but I know firsthand that things continue to get better if you are willing to continue working. You may well reach a point where continued therapy is no longer warranted, but practicing and building on what you're learned can continue regardless.

It is nice to realize that the stigma of seeking help for a mental illness is much diminished today. My sense is that some stigma remains, but it is much less severe than in previous times and not to be concerned with. As

Lady Gaga has said, "We can no longer afford to be silenced by stigma or stymied by misguided ideas that portray these conditions (i.e., mental illness) as a matter of weakness or moral failing. There is a lot of shame attached to mental illness …but this is a part of me and that's OK."

Should you need even more valid support for beginning or continuing a therapy regime, remember this:

> **No one who matters cares.**
> **No one who cares matters.**

——◦——

INCREASE YOUR CHANCES OF SUCCESS…EXPONENTIALLY!

The idea behind choosing therapy comes down to this: Why not try to reach your goals more expeditiously? If you are in pain, wouldn't you want the best option for ridding yourself of the suffering, and wouldn't you like that pain to end as soon as possible? Accepting and receiving professional help should be the best way to accomplish this.

If you are currently having trouble and not progressing in terms of managing or moving beyond certain issues, aren't you interested in getting as close as possible to your potential for peace and happiness in the shortest possible time, thereby leaving yourself with the maximum amount of time possible in which to enjoy your improved life? In therapy sessions people are working through issues in order to enjoy richer, fuller lives; and what a benefit that can be!

If you're still having difficulty wrapping your mind around the idea of being comfortable with seeing a therapist, think of it as seeing someone on a regular basis who allows you to fully relax and say anything and everything on your mind. It's a blessing to have somebody like that, and a rare thing indeed to have the opportunity to do this. And, after having aired what's troubling or confusing you, hopefully you will receive non-judgmental feedback, advice, assistance, direction, suggestions for changes, acceptance, validation, and understanding. You may never have experienced such things fully, and it's a godsend when you do.

Therapy is the one place where you can, and should, drop all pretenses, excuses, and defenses, and do your absolute best to be completely open to positive suggestions and realizations of needed changes. For all of the above reasons, it is easy to see why, overall, therapy can be a freeing and positive experience.

THE INFINITE ONION

For those of you who decide to take this leap forward, you should know there may be times along the way when therapy is not comfortable or enjoyable. We all wish it were easy, but no one can ever promise us only rainbows and unicorns, right? You may have to deal with troubling and difficult topics. But going through these is the best way forward.

Just hang in there despite such times! You will be very glad you did, both along the way and in the end. Just keep communicating and keep doing the work. And for those of you who decide to follow this path, please see Appendix C for further thoughts.

As mentioned above, you also may have heard the idea that therapy is like peeling an onion and that there can be many different layers of understanding and progress relating to a specific issue. Don't discount this or think that with your first revelation you have gotten to the core. Possibly you have, but there may still be additional layers to uncover. I have been surprised in the last five years about the lessons and further learning that were still available to me. I'm not sure a person ever gets to the end—and so for me, therapy seems to be an infinite onion. But with peeling off and exposing each and every layer comes a fuller, richer, more peaceful, and happier life!

MENTAL MASSAGE

It may help you to think of therapy as a mental massage. Many of us treat ourselves routinely to body massages, just as we go to get haircuts or manicures. If you do massages to get the physical kinks out and feel better physically, why not get the mental kinks out as well with therapy, a mental massage which might induce some temporary discomfort as your therapist works with you, but ultimately makes you feel amazing and relaxed.

Don't you care about your life, your relationships, your career, and your overall happiness at least as much as, or more than, your looks or your nails? What could be more important? You can become more relaxed, and feel stronger, more resilient, complete, and capable.

The truth of the matter for me is that I am not at all sure I would even be alive today without the work I have done due to therapy. I realize that is an extreme statement; but I have had two heart issues and a TIA already, and I'm not at all sure what the effects of extreme anxiety and stress would have been without this kind of work on my mental and emotional health. However, what I am sure about is my life would not be even close to being as wonderful as it is now without the efforts that came about in connection with my therapy.

In the end, your happiness is intertwined with how you deal with the stuff life presents. Therapy can greatly help you with this!

CHAPTER 36

STRATEGY – CONSIDER THIS LIFE-CHANGER

FOR YEARS, I LAUGHED many times at the slogan of one of the big U.S. chemical companies, DuPont: "A better life through chemistry!" But in my fifties, my mental health turnaround got a huge boost; it was at this time that I finally recognized and accepted that the best way, and about the only option I had not previously tried, to combat my brain chemistry imbalances was to offset them with medicine (i.e., other chemicals) to put things back in balance.

Some people initially reject the thought of going on medication for their imbalances because they think taking the medication will change who they are—in other words, medication will somehow change their inner being.

For me the reality was I had been letting fear run, and ruin, my life for many, many years. I chose the option of medicine not to change myself, but to let myself get closer to my true self and potential.

BREAKTHROUGH!

Accepting medication as a necessary and welcome component of my life was quite a breakthrough for me. For over three decades I actively resisted taking medicine even though my doctors had suggested doing so and prescribed it for me. Why? My reasons were several:

> First, I had an irrational fear of getting hooked on the medicine or other drugs or dying due to not being able to respond in an emergency, should one arise. This erroneous fear caused me to suffer needlessly. Upon taking medicine, my world changed

dramatically and quickly for the better, something that could have happened over thirty years earlier.

> Second, I had high expectations for myself and a very determined nature. I did not easily give up on curing myself completely on my own with therapy and my own self-improvement efforts.

> Third, I had a very busy personal and professional life, and while I was doing my absolute best to get over my issues, I hesitated to take meds in fear of their effects or side-effects. A mistake.

> Fourth, until this time in my life, there had always been other options to try, other possibilities.

> Finally, I had a therapist at the time who was very persuasive, and I came to accept that the effects of prescription drugs were relatively benign.

When appropriate, medicine can be the single best and most readily impactful tool many people use to fight those chemical imbalances in the brain which cause disruptive feelings such as pain, misery, anger, upset, and anxiety. The impact of the intervention of medicine on the body is amazing.

The idea behind its use is not to change yourself, but to just let yourself get as close as possible to achieving your potential. Not only can you be more effective and capable, but you may also exhibit more loving actions and experience increased pleasure, calm, and contentment. You can be more engaged with life and others. I definitely do not recommend that you follow in my footsteps and wait as long as I did to explore this path.

Several decades ago, a man named Werner Erhard founded est, an early self-actualization and empowerment movement. One of the small, less consequential things Erhard was known for was his ability to "disappear headaches" (cure them). Yet, there is a story that during a tour of his home one time, a sharp-eyed visitor spied a bottle of aspirin in his medicine cabinet and good-naturedly asked why Erhard would use aspirin if he could make headaches disappear without medication. The answer was that even though he did have this ability, sometimes a person just wants an aspirin—the other way takes too long. That works for me!

It is extremely important to find a qualified professional to prescribe the appropriate medication and dosage, which may be for the long term or used in the short term along with your other efforts to get over a particularly difficult bump in the road. Only a doctor can prescribe such medication, and they will want to monitor you at least a few times a year. Over my 70-year history in this field, I have found that psychiatrists seem to do less of the actual therapy work with anxiety patients these days, while psychologists and social workers are doing increasingly more.

As mentioned above, the fact that you may be experiencing anxiety of one kind or another is, in fact, an important warning sign that your mind and body are trying to get you to recognize—that there is a disturbance in the force! Something is wrong! "Danger, Will Robinson, danger!" Please listen to what your mind and body are trying to tell you!

<hr>

DON'T LEAVE HOME WITHOUT IT

I have adopted another advertising slogan to refer to any medicine prescribed for a person's mental health: "Don't leave home without it." (Thank you, American Express). This is especially true and pertinent if a person might be susceptible to sudden emotional swings, like panic attacks.

While you may not believe this until you try taking some medication, the reality is that just knowing that you have medication which will help you quickly can help you totally avoid an unpleasant experience. Having appropriate help in your pocket or purse can make an incredible difference, and let you ride out untoward feelings or even eliminate them!

I have had some of the worst times in my life when I had thought I was strong and not in need of my medication. For instance, I had trips and vacations on which I did not bring medication, and I ended up without it when I had a critical need. The trips turned out to be disasters of the highest order.

Your goal can be to stop walking around at the effect of a poor mental outlook or faulty thinking patterns that can negatively affect your enjoyment of life! Look into correcting such things with medication if the healthcare professionals in your life advise you to do so. It can make a dramatic difference in and for your entire life.

———◦———

BAD MEDICINE

A word about taking nonprescription drugs, as opposed to prescription medicine ...

I have a tremendous amount of empathy for anyone who has sufficient mental or physical pain that they try to avoid it by using alcohol, nicotine, or nonprescription drugs. Having had a lot of pain and anxiety issues, I have an appreciation for what a person might choose to do in order to avoid it; but this is definitely NOT the way to live. When it comes to reaching for alcohol or nonprescription drugs, they make for "bad medicine." They may be tempting, but they also can cause way more problems than they fix, with some making a person more prone to anger or depression, for example. Choosing to manage your issue with these methods is a way of really not dealing with the basic problems at all. It is infinitely better to seek help in other ways than to use these substances to mask the issues you are facing.

As you know by now, I have never pursued nonprescription drugs to combat or distract from my problems, as I had too many control issues to ever take a chance with illegal drugs or some of the more common legal ones, like nicotine or alcohol. Prescribed medicine is a healthier and more productive way of dealing with these problems. A hundred years ago, we lacked medications targeted to help deal with anxiety, emotional issues, or mental illness; today we have these and over time the medications have become more effective and varied. There are more options available and they work better. There are different medical classifications, but on a layman's level the different medications fall into two basic types:

> Those taken daily.
> Those used on an as needed basis.

As to the latter, I call these **"ICE"** meds – taken **In Case of Emergency**. It is always great to catch yourself before you escalate to a full-blown panic or anxiety attack. You might be using the strategies and techniques in this book to reduce these feelings, but we all know that spikes occur from time to time; and it can take no more than a second or two for your emotions to get out of control. Sometimes you are at 15 on a scale of 1-10 before you are able to start doing anything to help yourself, and **ICE** meds can make a huge difference in such situations. Keep them handy.

CHAPTER 37

STRATEGY – DON'T COMPLAIN WITHOUT CHANGE!

"A good scapegoat is nearly as welcome as a solution to the problem."
– Author Unknown

THIS IDEA OF NOT COMPLAINING without suggesting changes ties into another of my favorite goals, which is to never have the same problem twice. There is an old, well-known question:

> **If you don't have time to do it right, when will you have time to do it over?**

There is a world of wisdom in the above. And while it may not be possible in all cases to permanently solve problems, I do believe it is the correct objective to try. Striving for the right outcome can help engender your creativity and change your thinking from negative to positive! This is not to say that the same problem won't crop up from time to time or that you will always be successful in ridding yourself of repeat problems, but it is a good mindset to adopt. When you see yourself dealing with problems you have had before and find you are definitely not enjoying the process, try to come up with a permanent solution.

> **Why continue to deal with SSDD (Same Stuff, Different Day)? You are better than that!**

If you are able to adopt the never-complain-without-change mentality, you will begin to pull yourself out of negativity and towards creativity. Just thinking about what needs to be done and looking for ways to change something in the future may bring some resolution to the problem, and this reinforces the advantages of having a positive mental attitude about solving problems.

Finally, this strategy makes use of the idea that just taking action—doing something, almost ANYTHING—may help rid you of stress and other negative feelings. However, lest you think that I am a male version of Mary Poppins, let me assure you that I fully understand that, as humans, it is almost impossible not to be grumpy, to complain from time to time, or to be negative. Let yourself be human if that happens, but keep asking what you can change to make the situation better, limit the onslaught and reach of negative feelings, and get yourself back to a positive track sooner. Keep in mind, though, that trying to make changes may seem scary at first and that to do this, you may need to be vulnerable.

> **Vulnerability is the courage to show up and be seen and heard when you can't control the outcome, taking the chance of making mistakes – large or small – and risking that it all will go to $#!@.**

Think about how you will feel if you do not take the risk and strive to make a change: You may regret it forever! As Dr. Brown, the author of *Daring Greatly*, says,

"Vulnerability can be terrifying and dangerous. But it's never as terrifying or dangerous as getting to the end of your life and asking why you never showed up, why you never tried."

———◉———

IT DOESN'T HAVE TO BE HARD

Heeding this strategic advice need not be a long, painful mental process. To a large degree, I'm suggesting a relatively quick, first-thought mindset change.

Maybe the solution you will propose is serious; maybe it is funny, crazy, illegal, etc.—whatever! The important thing is that your potential solution comes from a place of positivity and looking forward rather than reminiscing endlessly or ruminating about what went wrong and how often this has happened to you before. Also, coming up with almost any solution will help keep your mind on positive outcomes.

Get away from a negative mindset, be creative, and even have some fun. It can make a world of difference.

CHAPTER 38

STRATEGY – PEG YOUR HAPPINESS ON WHAT YOU CAN CONTROL

WHENEVER POSSIBLE PEG your happiness to what you can control. It is unproductive and quite fruitless to set your happiness on, say, winning a million dollars in the lottery since you are basing your joy on something completely out of your hands, other than buying the tickets, of course.

Choose to base your happiness and dreams on something that you can be responsible for and achieve through practical means. Take the writing of this book, for example: My goal here was to write it and offer my help to others. This was something I myself could fulfill. Doing it has already brought me much peace and joy. Writing the book was completely within my control, and I will feel wonderful to have completed it. If people decide to use my book as a doorstop rather than something that could make their lives better, or not even look at it or purchase it, that's up to them: I will have offered my gift and tried to help, and I intend to feel fulfilled no matter what happens after that. If I were to peg my happiness regarding this book on changing the world or another person, having a bestseller, or any of a host of other goals that are beyond my control, I might well be setting myself up for major disappointment. Sure, I truly would like to help others with this book ... but in my mind that will be the icing on the cake, or as we say in Louisiana, lagniappe. I cannot control how or whether people will use what I have to offer. I have pegged my goal and happiness to what I can control.

For another example, let's say we have two guys ... we will call them Hal and Don ... both of whom work hard, want a successful career, and would like to be promoted. The men are equally competent. The only difference is that Don's only goal is to get the promotion, whereas Hal has a more nuanced goal. Although he wants to be promoted as badly as Don, his focus is on doing his best to deserve the promotion. Now let's look at the possible outcomes. If both Don and Hal get promoted, they will, of course, both be happy. But, if Don does not get promoted, he will probably feel disappointed. Hal, on the other hand, may well feel less disappointed and possibly rest happily in the knowledge that he did, in fact, do all he could to deserve the promotion even if it did not come. He can feel validated because he took responsibility for the goal in terms of what he could do to influence the outcome. He took charge of what he could control to affect change and at least achieved that part of the goal.

Here are two questions that I will leave you with for this section:

> **If you can avoid it, why would you ever want to set your goals on things beyond your control?**

> **Isn't that a recipe for disappointment?**

CHAPTER 39
STRATEGY – JOT IT DOWN

WHEN I WAS YOUNG, I was able to keep many things straight in my mind and I did not have to rely on writing things down. But when I began my first full-time job after college, I became overwhelmed with the volume of things I had to keep in mind and handle. I ended up having horrible nightmares about imaginary problems related to work; and I realized that, in a way, I was overtaxing my mind by trying to remember too many things. It was at that point that I began to make notes, and I learned doing so both cleared and calmed my mind.

Jotting things down also was extremely important to me whenever I got overly anxious as I was very afraid I would forget something important that could later serve as a clue to a therapist as to the issues I was having. The last thing I wanted was to perpetuate my self-torture by forgetting to discuss something important in a session. As long as I tried to keep the memory of important things or discoveries just in my head, I felt I had to repeat them over and over to ensure that I would not forget anything. This kept me trapped in the anxiety associated with those thoughts. At this point I started to make notes and subsequently discovered I was able to let go of the thoughts after writing them down. Since they were captured on paper for whatever, whenever, and wherever I needed them, I no longer needed to obsess over them and keep them circulating in my mind. Now I could begin to relax much more easily because I had stopped the vicious thought cycle in my head! The notes helped me clear my mind so I could be more creative and productive; the process allowed my mind to move on, whereas it would or could not move on without my making notes.

We all have hundreds of thoughts each day, many of which are useless or nonproductive and which warrant no further attention. However, for the ones that we really want to remember and the ones you feel are important for one reason or another, it is invaluable to jot them down.

Jotting things down, either by writing, typing, or dictating, does a number of positive things simultaneously:

> Helps to stop the mind from racing or jumping from one thing to another.

> Soothes and comforts the mind, since it no longer has to keep working to remember something.

> Releases the mind because it is able to set aside those thoughts now.

> Gets any negative, angry, hate-filled, depressing, and/or anxious thoughts out of your head. You are now venting.

> Reinforces that you are trying to change certain negative and unproductive behaviors or thought patterns.

> Puts you in a position to analyze or discuss these past thoughts ... or you could just let them go.

Being a good note-taker also proved to be a strength in college, on the job, as well as in daily life. For me, there is absolutely no way to remember everything without notes; and once having taken some notes, it was relatively easy to work out a filing and reminder system, one that has proved to be invaluable to me in numerous ways. For example, using it in my business life provided me with a very complete set of business files which were in demand by others who wanted to check on historical and other substantive factual matters.

Yes, I do realize that there is a cost to the practice of making notes—it takes time and effort. But I know that for me, the benefits outweigh the cost by a huge margin! Not only does it help me concentrate better on the matter at hand while having information available for later, but also having the notes frees my mind to think of new or related matters.

Jotting things down is a skill worth cultivating over your whole life! And with all the features of our modern phones, the taking, filing, and retrieval of notes is much easier.

CHAPTER 40
STRATEGY –NOTICE YOUR BODY'S EARLY WARNING SYSTEM

FOR MANY YEARS, MY body has tried to alert me when something was getting out of whack. For example, if I noticed my peripheral vision was diminishing so that I was aware of only a very limited field of vision, it was a red flag that I was about to have some sort of anxiety attack. Another warning of an imminent attack was when I noticed I had absolutely no sense of humor. I have had people come into my office and tell a joke and I just blankly stare at them with no comprehension of what was funny. Finally, I can generally notice my mind racing and jumping from one thought to another before I am aware of excess stress or anxiety. Red Flags! Actually, I am grateful for my body's early warning system, and that I have raised my awareness of what is going on in my body so I can benefit from these helpful signals.

If you too can notice the actions or reactions your body generally uses to signal that you are headed for trouble mentally or emotionally, you can take corrective action sooner. You can engage in a strategy or technique which hopefully will keep your issue from blossoming and allow you to avoid any major negative effects. Maybe, like me, you might choose to do the one or more of the following:

> Take a break,

> Meditate,

> Do some deep breathing,

> Say your affirmations to distract yourself and increase your self-confidence,

> Listen to music that is soothing and relaxing,

> Think of an emotional story,

> Call a good friend to talk things out and enjoy their support,

> Take a walk,

> Exercise (see next chapter),

> Take prescription meds that are appropriate for your condition or issue, or

> Any other strategy that calms you.

Whatever works! What you are doing by employing these strategies is, in all cases, to redirect your train of thought. Rather than continuing to chase your tail in a downward spiral that ends in a very negative space, you can intervene and break the pattern. You can focus on positive thoughts and emotions. How fantastic it would be for you, through your newfound awareness, to be able to mitigate or completely eliminate what would otherwise be a very unpleasant experience!

CHAPTER 41
STRATEGY – PEACE THROUGH EXERCISE

WHAT IS GOOD FOR THE mind is also good for the body, and vice versa. If you exercise to strengthen your body, you will almost certainly also reduce your stress, stress hormones, anxiety, and adrenaline. It's peace through exercise.

When you engage in exercise, be gratified by the knowledge that people who exercise regularly generally live longer, feel better, and are more productive. That's a LOT of bang for your exercise buck and should be good news for all those folks who like multitasking so much.

Exercise is a positive, all-natural, non-addictive, non-pharmaceutical aid in reducing and controlling anxiety! It's an activity that is hard to fault, if done within reason and after consulting with your healthcare professional, of course.

THE BENEFITS ARE REAL

To monitor your actual progress, consider purchasing a heart rate and/or blood pressure monitor. These will show you in real-time what your heart rate and blood pressure are, and you can see their decreases over time with a set intensity or duration of exercise. Employing such devices makes it easy to monitor what is going on with your body and helps if you want to push yourself to run that extra mile, do more crunches, or lift a bit more than usual.

Another thing to consider is a good pedometer, such as Fitbit, smartwatch, or phone. These portable electronic devices track not only your steps but also other useful metrics. You can also use them to monitor your sleep so you have an independent gauge as to how peacefully or restlessly you may be sleeping.

Remember this:

> ### › A bad day of exercise is better than a good day on the sofa!

So just get up, get out, or go to your home gym; and do something active.

When you do exercise, focus your mind on what you can do and what you have done. Do not employ self-flagellation about what you may not have done or what you can no longer do, like being unable to play tennis or bike if you are older and your joints are arthritic. Just do what you can and feel good about it!

Physical activity seems to always clear the mind and allow fresh ideas to bubble up. I know that I've had a number of good ideas which would never have come to me had I stayed at my desk and worked on the normal activities of the day. I don't know how the brain actually works, but it certainly feels like I've turned a situation over to my subconscious and put my mind in neutral while I exercise. Then when my subconscious has something it feels is worthy to say, it coughs up the idea like a cat might cough up a hairball—but in a much nicer way, of course.

CHAPTER 42
STRATEGY – SLEEP IT OFF

ONE OF MY PRIMARY SYMPTOMS during an anxiety episode was an inability to get to or stay asleep, so any admonition to "just go to sleep" virtually made my head explode. If I could sleep, I would not have been anxious, and if I were not anxious, I would be able to sleep!

However, I do know that for others this may not be the case. For instance, some people who get depressed often sleep as an escape from their issue. There are many health benefits of getting enough good, restful sleep and the correct amount of sleep will help you maintain or regain your equilibrium.

My mental health can be negatively impacted by a less-than-normal amount of sleep. Others tell me I get grouchy and negative when I'm tired—something I am actually aware of in myself. I have to fight the urge to be snarky at times when I am fatigued, and a lack of adequate sleep definitely darkens my outlook on the world.

It is well accepted that mental and physical health benefits abound upon getting sufficient restorative sleep, and your eating habits can be improved. So if you are experiencing anxiety issues while not getting adequate sleep, this is an area to consider addressing. There are tremendous sleep aids on the market, including the following:

> Setting sleep routines, such as when to begin the process, when to turn off the lights, and when to get up.

> Having the proper sleep environment, including the degree of light, your preferred room temperature, preferred pillows, and the use of heated blankets.

> Seeing sleep disorder specialists.

> Checking for sleep apnea.

> Reading before sleep to relax your body and mind ... especially positive relaxing stories.

> Listening to white noise or nature sounds generators.

> Meditating.

> Repeating your own affirmations silently.

Try a few of these techniques and see what works best for you. Sleep well!

CHAPTER 43
STRATEGY: BE SENSE-ITIVE

TOO FEW OF US ARE SUFFICIENTLY aware of and grateful for our bodies and how they actually work. For example, it is through our senses that our minds interpret the world, making our senses extremely important for our survival and for how we think and feel.

Much like with technology and science, we can choose to use the abilities of our senses for good or evil. Let me explain. We can choose to use any or all of our five senses to give positive, uplifting, warm, fuzzy input to our minds, or we can use our senses in a way that makes our circumstances or environment seem darker and more dire. We can also consciously and deliberately employ the senses to help us get the hell out of our minds (literally and figuratively) as a helpful way to deal with anxiety, negative self-talk, disturbing emotions, and/or a bad attitude.

Manufacturers and advertisers appeal to the senses to manipulate us for their (nefarious?) marketing purposes. Consider these simple examples of using consumers' senses to sell them something:

> Real estate agents tell sellers to make chocolate chip cookies and then leave a plate of them out during an open house: The smell of freshly baked chocolate chip cookies will be appealing to potential buyers, touching them on a deep level and perhaps helping to influence them to make an offer.

> Sellers have adopted the science of neuro-linguistic programming to discover a potential buyer's dominant sense so a salesperson will know how to most effectively appeal to him or her. For example:

- Dominant Sense: Sales Approach - What The Salesman Emphasizes:
    - Sight: The look and the lines of a car and its interior or exterior.
    - Smell: The new car smell; the smell of the leather upholstery.
    - Touch: The feel of the leather upholstery; the feel of the steering wheel when driving the car and turning the wheel; the comfort of the interior seating and an ample amount of leg room.
    - Taste: Doughnut stores, steakhouses and restaurants might have their kitchen vents blow tempting smells to the parking lot or sidewalk to greet and lure in customers.
    - Hearing: The purr of a motor or the range of the sound system.

You too can employ your senses in ways to increase your sense of comfort, peace, and tranquility. The following are just a selection of suggestions; there are countless ways you can use each of your senses to benefit yourself.

> Sight:

Visualize some of your favorite places! Possibly you might enjoy thinking about times when you have been warm and relaxed (e.g., when you were on a beach), or when you have been active in a cool and delightful environment (e.g., hiking in a forest or gazing from the peak of a mountain). Try to actually go to one of these locations if it makes you feel better. The possibilities for visualization are virtually endless.

- Art. Think of a painting or sculpture that is so beautiful it moves you. Tour a museum and appreciate the different exhibits on display; if the museum tickets are expensive for your budget, check with your local library, as many will loan free museum passes to their patrons. Go to an artsy part of town and visit those stores that feature the art of local artists. Create a piece of art that brings you pleasure.

- Enjoy the many different, indescribable, and unique looks of nature, whether they be sunsets, sunrises, mountains, lakes, oceans, coastlines, rock formations, plants, etc.
- Gaze at pictures that show or elicit from you positive or calming emotions.
- Work to block out any negative outside stimuli and focus on something more pleasing to the mind and heart.

> Smell:

- Many people find the smell of lavender soothing, and a tremendous body of knowledge exists concerning the subject of aromatherapy, including essential oils, herbs, and so on. Place such smells around your home or apartment if they are pleasing to you.
    ○ The smell of coffee in the morning helps many people begin the day with a warm, fuzzy, positive, and motivating feeling.
    ○ Visualize or go somewhere to enjoy your specific favorite smells, whether it's the smoke arising from a campfire, the smell of a flower, or pine tree.

The key point is that smells trigger thoughts, thoughts trigger feelings, and feelings influence your life and moods. Actually, your mind is so very fast and complex that it literally jumps from smells to feelings, but the memories and thoughts have to be in there originally or there would be no way to explain why one person has a good feeling from a smell while the same smell might trigger a panic attack in another person.

> Touch:

- Touch tends to eliminate the feeling of isolation and let anxiety flow out of the body.

- Hold hands with a loved one.
- Get a massage or backrub.
- Pet a cat or dog (or llama, hamster, etc.!).

> Taste:

- Enjoy a favorite kind of coffee or tea, or a nice cup of hot chocolate.
- Take yourself out. Do you like Indian or Mexican food? Treat yourself and a friend to a meal featuring a kind of cuisine that you don't make at home. If your budget is an issue, find a recipe online for a dish that sounds great...and make it at home.
- Pamper yourself when you can; perhaps visit your parents if Mom's cooking is something you enjoy.
- Try something new: Add different flavors you haven't tried before. Cook something that uses spices like cardamon, cumin, and turmeric, and see if these tastes rock your boat.
- Become an herbivore. Pick up some herbs in the store or grow some, pick off a leaf, and try it. Do you prefer the taste of basil or mint? What dishes might you eat that you could add a basil leaf to? Try a margarita pizza, or fill a pitcher of water and let some mint sit in it for a few days...then enjoy drinking your flavored water.

> Hearing:

- Get an audiobook or podcast that features calm, deep voices...and listen.
- Get out of your home and enjoy the soothing and quite interesting sounds of nature, whether it's the ocean waves, the falling rain, birds calling to each other, or squirrels chattering away.
- Enjoy your favorite music. Music can affect your emotions, level of relaxation, and even your breathing if you sing along.

Here's another tip: If you are unable to physically get to the locations where you might enjoy the experiences generated by your senses, employ them in a meditation to help with relaxing.

⸻ ◉ ⸻

JUST IMAGINE...

How would you feel if you spent a day in the environment noted below:

You are surrounded by pictures and other items that bring warm, pleasant memories and feelings each time you see them. After enjoying the sight of these items, you walk outside and hear sounds (babbling streams, birds, crashing waves, etc.) that soothe and relax. Invigorated by the sounds of nature, you return inside and choose to listen to music which uplifts, encourages, comforts, and relaxes you. As you move about your home, you ensure you are engulfed in an atmosphere that is the temperature you enjoy and are surrounded by physical things including your family pet, which bring you pleasure and comfort. You keep smelling certain aromas, like chocolate chip cookies or roses, which bring back pleasing, wonderfully loving memories. You walk into your kitchen and are able to eat your favorite foods which not only nourish your body but satisfy any cravings you may have. If this were your day, wouldn't you feel amazing, and characterize it as a great day?

Now read the previous paragraph again and think about how you might feel if exactly the opposite feelings were experienced through each sense all day long. I know your answer here, and I definitely know mine: I am clear as to which option would lead to a more relaxed and positive mood.

Here's some more good news: The more you do positive visualization, the more you are training your mind to be at peace and positively inclined. And even better news: Many of the images and items are readily available to you via today's electronic age. But it is up to you to choose to surround yourself with the unique things that bring pleasure to your senses.

If I were you, I'd make that choice right now.

CHAPTER 44
STRATEGY – MAKE USE OF MUSIC

"Music expresses that which cannot be said and which cannot remain
silent."
– Victor Hugo
"Music has powers to soothe the savage beast!"
– Shakespeare

AS SHAKESPEARE JUST told us above, listening to music can make an enormous difference in a person's emotional state.

Listening to music that moves, comforts, or enlivens me is one of the first and most enjoyable and impactful techniques I came across to help dampen my anxious feelings. There was a point at which I realized that I could not simultaneously be anxious and be emotionally moved by music. If, when anxious thoughts began, I had the presence of mind to listen to good music, there was no longer a place in my mind for those anxious thoughts to exist. The two could not cohabitate.

This was a "Eureka" moment for me, and almost every day now I have music playing in the background regardless of what I am doing. When I concentrate on it, it focuses my mind, producing relaxing or enlivening mental images. And I believe that over time we get a subconscious benefit even if we are not aware of hearing the music. The music simply elevates our mood.

That certainly beats sitting around wondering if or when excess anxiety might strike.

EAR PEACE

Long ago, in the 1960's or 1970's—well before it was possible to accomplish technologically—I had an idea which I dubbed "Ear Peace." I asked a good friend of mine in the audio-visual equipment field if he knew of any way to have a receiver placed in the ear so a small transmitter could send music to it. At the time, there was no such equipment—but as you are undoubtedly aware, now this equipment is everywhere. With any cell phone and Bluetooth ear pods you can have your music with you anywhere and anytime 24/7/365.

It seems odd thinking back on Ear Peace and the fact that this was not even possible at one time ... a time period that seems like the technological Dark Ages now. Today you can wake up and go through all phases of your day with music playing near you, whether you choose to have it in your car, your phone, a remote speaker, a record player, wireless ear pods, headset, and so on. As someone who longed for just a fraction of this long before it was possible, it is hard for me to even describe how impactful this has been for me and might be for you!

My favorite kinds of music are:

> Soothing

> Music that touches or moves me emotionally

> Loving

> Patriotic

> Uplifting or inspiring

> Upbeat and enlivening

> Music that gives people "happy feet" (it makes them want to dance or just get moving!).

But these are just the categories I've discovered that work for me: Your goal is to find what kinds of music make it difficult or impossible for you to entertain unhappy thoughts or dismal moods.

Use this strategy as often as you can and keep the music going as long as possible.

REMEMBER #1

The strategy of using music to focus the mind on positive feelings reminds me of a part of the movie "City Slickers" in which Jack Palance plays Curly, the trail boss. At one point Curly explains that the secret of life is always remembering what is number one. Or, as Curly might say,

"The most important thing is to remember the most important thing!"

So, what is that most important thing for you? It could be any of the following examples, or something completely different:

> Gratitude
> Joy
> Love
> Family
> Peace
> Perspective
> Forgiveness
> Helping others
> Using your power of choice in the best way.

Give the question some thought and settle on something that feels right for you. You can change your mind about your number one thing as often as you like, but hopefully you will ultimately find the one that really works for you. And then you can use ever-present music to help you get to and keep that good feeling, thought, or perspective ever present in your mind.

If you do this, it can make your day much more enjoyable. You will be blocking out much of the anxiety and noise while allowing a pleasing thought that's of the highest priority to fill you.

Give it a try the next time you are down or begin to feel anxious. Choose several of your favorite songs, or ones from the lists below; play them for a while and really listen. They can help keep your mind where you want it, letting you feel really good and keeping you from being upset.

———— ◆ ————

FAVORITE TUNES

Some of the songs that work especially well for me are the following: Emotional, calming, patriotic, and/or soothing—

> "Lean on Me" by Anne Murray

> "Hallelujah" by Jeff Buckley, Rufus Wainwright, or k.d. lang

> "Bridge over Troubled Waters" by Simon and Garfunkel or Elvis Presley

> "The Rose" by Bette Midler

> "Stand by Me" by John Lennon

> "Let It Be" by The Beatles

> "That Summer" by Garth Brooks

> "Sunshine on My Shoulders" by John Denver

> "Spirit in the Sky" by Elton John

> "Help Me Make It Through the Night" by Willie Nelson

> "Wind Beneath My Wings" by Bette Midler

> "You'll Never Walk Alone" by American Tenors

> "The Windmills of Your Mind" by James Galway or Andre Rieu

> "Memory" from the play "Cats"

> "Amazing Grace" by Anne Murray, American Tenors, Elvis Presley, Judy Collins, or others

> "An American Trilogy" by Elvis Presley

> "Blind Man in the Bleachers" by Kenny Starr

> "The First Time Ever I Saw Your Face" by Celine Dion or others

> "The Greatest" by Kenny Rogers

> "I Will Always Love You" by Whitney Houston

> "The Impossible Dream" by Elvis Presley or others

> "Because You Loved Me" by Celine Dion or others

> "Little Drummer Boy" by Mary J. Blige

> "My Way" by Frank Sinatra

> "Softly and Tenderly" by Anne Murray

> "Belleau Wood" by Garth Brooks

> "Hero" by Mariah Carey

> "How Great Thou Art" by Elvis Presley

> "Just a Closer Walk with Thee" by Anne Murray

> "Scarlet Ribbons" by The Kingston Trio

> "We Shall Be Free" by Garth Brooks

> "My Heart Will Go On" by Celine Dion

> "Here Comes That Rainbow Again" by Kris Kristofferson or others

> "I Hope You'll Dance" by Lee Ann Womack

> "I Came to Believe" by Johnny Cash

Enlivening—

> "I Will Survive" by Gloria Gaynor
> "What Doesn't Kill You Makes You Stronger" by Julie Stone or F. Rocha
> "Come on Over" by Shania Twain
> "Walk a Mile in My Shoes" by Elvis Presley
> "Johnny B. Goode" by Chuck Berry or Elvis Presley
> "Proud Mary" by Tina Turner or Elvis Presley
> "Joy to the World" by Three Dog Night
> "Lay Down Sally" by Eric Clapton
> "Up Around the Bend" by Credence Clearwater Revival
> "You Don't Mess Around with Jim" by Jim Croce
> "Down at the Twist and Shout" by Mary Chapin Carpenter
> "Footloose" from the soundtrack of the movie by the same name
> "You're Still the One" by Shania Twain
> "Put a Little Love in Your Heart" by Anne Murray
> "Bad Moon Rising" by Creedence Clearwater Revival
> "Travelling Band" by Creedence Clearwater Revival
> "This Little Light of Mine" by The Kingston Trio
> "Don't Stop Believin'" by Journey
> "Holding Out for a Hero" from the soundtrack of "Footloose"
> "Let Your Love Flow" by The Bellamy Brothers
> "Go Big or Go Home" by American Authors

PART VI

NEXT STEPS

PART VI - OVERVIEW

MY HOPE FOR YOU IS that at this point you understand your anxiety issues better and feel ready to take concrete steps to improve your life. The purpose of this last part of the book is to help you do exactly that. I want to help you avoid certain problems as you work your way towards the beneficial changes you desire; and while it is always up to you to decide when and how to change, hopefully working together I can help you increase your success in having the best life possible.

CHAPTER 45
PICK YOUR PATH

DECIDING ON YOUR STRATEGIES FIRST

Having gotten to this stage, you may want to build as many strategies as possible into your life as soon as possible. Well, I suggest you take your time and remember that you can't learn or implement them all at once, especially at first. Plus, it behooves you to figure out your own go-to list.

Change, cull, add to, and tailor my list and ideas; they are here just to get you started. The strategies included in this book get and keep me grounded—but you are free to do things your way. Just remember your goal of reducing or eliminating your anxiety and negative emotions as much as possible.

I'd like you to be aware that if one or a group of strategies fails you when you use it sporadically, that does not mean it is not for you or does not work. It just may indicate that you need to use it more often and to build it over time into your daily life. Hopefully, you will find there is much less room for fear, regret, anxiety, doubt, or worry if you employ the strategies daily and become able to engulf yourself in gratitude, forgiveness, contentment, and peace. The wonderful thing is that you don't have to wait for relief and improvement until after hitting a critical mass. You can have a gradual but significant improvement, in proportion to your efforts.

WHICH APPROACH IS GOING TO BE BEST FOR YOU?

I want you to know that there are significant differences between using and living the strategies as you move forward. Specifically:

> Using the Strategies: Taking this approach allows you to go about your life with a list of strategies in your back pocket or in your head, which you pull out to employ if, as, and when they may be needed. This is likely to be what you hoped to get from this book. With this approach you lead your life to the fullest and richest level you're capable of without regularly employing the strategies. If you were to feel an increase in sadness, anger, shame, anxiety, or other negative emotions or thoughts, you would simply start employing one or more of the strategies you think might work best or which you've gotten results from in the past.

Doing this is a little like carrying your Superman suit (a.k.a., your strategies) with you at all times in your briefcase or purse for when it is needed. If trouble comes, you look for the phone booth in which to don that suit, knowing that if you use your strategic powers soon enough—e.g., before the bad guys shoot bullets at you—those powers will protect you. You have to get to the telephone booth before the bullets fly, however; and those phone booths are sometimes hard to locate these days. Plus, there may be some fumbling with buttons or zippers, etc., that hinder your ability to immediately get your powers in play. (And exactly where were the buttons or zippers on Superman's suit?!) Nonetheless, this is a good approach and a huge improvement over your situation before you earned your Superman suit!

Using the strategies as just described may completely work for you in your life—but it also may not. If, for example, anxiety and depression get a head start on your use of your strategies to combat them, using the strategies may provide results more slowly, and may prove less effective ... or not effective at all. If you find you are not satisfied with the quality of life you achieve this way, then you can increase your success by living the strategies—the most effective approach by far.

> Living the Strategies: Living the strategies helps you make changes to your life so issues neither occur in the first place nor rise up over time and bite you in the rear end. Think of living

the strategies as using them 24/7 rather than not employing them until and unless you feel they are needed.

What does this look like? You eat, sleep, breathe, work, and play in your Superman suit—so you are always ready, always protected. This provides the maximum possible bullet proof protection; and when those projectiles begin to fly, they simply bounce off of you. Here, for example, you build strategies you find helpful into your daily schedule regardless of how you feel or think each day. Perhaps exercise and meditation appeal to you. If you do these regularly each day, even when not on the cusp of a panic attack, you may well find that the normal events that previously caused you anxiety are much easier to deal with, and that you can do so calmly.

Think of using vs living the strategies in this analogous way: For weight management, many of us wait for the scale to give us unwelcome news, and then we mend our ways for a little while until we get back to an acceptable weight; only to repeat the cycle all too often. You could think of this as "using the strategies," because any good nutritionist will tell you that you have to change your eating habits permanently if you want the best long-term results. The nutritionist's advice would be an example of actually "living the strategies."

Another good way to think about the difference between using and living the strategies is to think of going to the dentist for a painful root canal or extraction procedure. Many of us would have the procedure and then take some sort of pain medicine to reduce the inevitable aching. This would be analogous to using the strategies. On the other hand, some people would take the medicine before going to the dentist. They will fortify their system in advance, not have to play catch-up with the pain, and generally have a much easier and more pain free day. Many dentists recommend that you take an OTC pain reliever prior to arriving for any invasive dental work so that it kicks in before the pain is actually there. This is living the strategies. We all know the pain is coming, right? Why not keep it to a minimum?

———◉———

DECISION-TIME!

Many strategies have been presented throughout this book with the primary focus of having you, the reader, decide which work best in your life and will allow you to reduce stress and anxiety while increasing happiness and peace. You may choose to live the strategies that work best for you, thereby employing them on a daily basis regardless of your emotional state. If meditation in the early morning before the bustle of getting the family off to school, or before you go to your job works best for you, then living this strategy would mean that you are meditating before even knowing whether the kids are particularly hyper that day or the boss is in a foul mood. If you choose the "using" version of this strategy, then meditation would only occur sometime after your stress level begins to rise. You may choose to experiment with a combination of both. You may enjoy an early morning meditation but wait to see how your day goes before deciding whether to meditate again in the evening or go for a run.

You also can multi-task and employ many strategies in your daily life—something that becomes easy with just a little bit of practice. I came from a zero-level of experience with all of the strategies, but I am now at a place where I've been using a number of them simultaneously for over 60 years. My advice is:

> **Work toward achieving a competence level with your strategies such that, even if or when you have a problem, it's NOT a problem.**

———◉———

CAPTAIN YOUR SHIP

As I write this, I am 80 years old and have spent a large part of my discretionary time over a number of years getting to this point in the book after achieving my goals for peace, relaxation, and productivity in life. I hope that by this time on our journey together you not only see some things about life more clearly, but you also understand that your future is much more in your own hands than it may have seemed before beginning this book.

Remember these thoughts as you proceed and progress on your path:

> "Do not pray to be safe, unhurt, or for there never to be a dark time. Stuff will happen! Accept that you will not get safe passage. Hurt will come, you will not always be safe, the world is not fair, and the darkness comes to us all from time to time. Instead, pray to be a good captain of your ship – to be able to steer your way through the storms which are sure to come. Pray to see clearly in the night. There will be many traumas, upsets, storms, and difficult situations. The best you can have is to be an able captain of your ship and steer through them." (*Transforming Trauma* by James Finley and Caroline Myss)

> "Life isn't about waiting for the storm to pass. It's about learning how to dance in the rain." Vivian Greene, Seattle born writer.

> And finally, my favorite therapist told me, "You can't stop the waves, but you can learn to surf."

You _are_ the captain, you _can_ dance in the rain, and you _can_ greatly improve your surfing skills. Have at it!

And remember that my wish for you is to have a full and exciting life that allows you to feel both satisfied and proud. We all follow our own individual paths through life, and I hope this book will make your journey easier. It is never too soon to begin and never too late to achieve your success. So never give in and never give up.

Have a spectacular life!

YOUR COMMENTS

YOUR COMMENTS ABOUT the offerings in this book are extremely valuable and of interest to me; and I would appreciate any and all thoughts you may have—positive, negative, or simply informative.

Please send your comments to: BTUTCOMMENTS@GMAIL.COM. Thanks in advance for providing these!

- HWS

APPENDIX A

A LIFETIME WELL SPENT: INTERESTS, ADVENTURES, AND REWARDS

I THINK THAT BEFORE you accept advice from someone, it is usually best to know something about the person. In that vein, I offer some background information on my life history and interests that will give you some further context about where I am coming from so you can better evaluate and trust the source of this book.

WHAT I'VE CHOSEN TO DO

To some people, it may seem that my life has been rather unusual. For example, I am not a huge fan of fishing, hunting, boating, golfing, recreational flying, or gambling, although I have enjoyed dabbling in most of these briefly. Nor am I an aficionado of the fine arts such as ballet, opera, classical music, or even much of the art world. Not surprisingly, I have spent relatively little time in museums.

While I use prescription and over the counter medications, I have never used illegal or other questionable non-prescription drugs of any kind; and I have absolutely no appreciation of wine, beer, or stronger versions of alcohol. Consequently, I haven't drunk alcohol to any significant degree, and I have never been drunk. I have probably spent less than an hour cumulatively throughout my life in bars; I have imbibed less than ¼ of a beer cumulatively throughout my life, and even less wine. I do enjoy a few (1-2) mixed drinks a year, but only if they are such that I can't taste the alcohol. I can feel the alcohol on the very first sip of a drink. Simply put, while I have nothing against alcohol per se, I very much prefer to chew my calories!

So just think of what could be accomplished if you tried every day (and I mean really tried - to the very best of your ability) to achieve other goals and pursue other interests than those mentioned above. That is what I have chosen to do ever since I was a teen, and these choices have left me free to concentrate on and pursue the other areas of my life which I felt were critical to my overall goals.

I have listed below achievements attained in my life thus far. They give me a sense of pride; but not to be overly dramatic, the list would have been much shorter if I had not sought out solutions to cope with my extreme anxiety and panic attacks. My choices have allowed me to participate in and/or help achieve the following:

> Honor student, class president, and student body president in high school.

> First (or very close) in my class in high school, college, and graduate school, with close to a 4.0 gpa throughout.

> Representative of my undergraduate university at a national convention on business and manufacturing.

> Awarded BBA, MBA, and CPA designations.

> Member of a number of honorary fraternities in college as well as one regular social fraternity.

> Married twice with two wonderful children from each marriage (ages of roughly 58, 56, and twins at 30 as of this writing – I am an even half-century older than my youngest children!).

> Practiced public accounting for 6 years at one of the world's finest international firms.

> Successful second career as a Chief Financial Officer for 39 years with a group of privately owned companies; I was responsible for the accounting, tax, and IT departments. I also headed up

all borrowing activities and progressed from a one-lender, $16 million facility in my early career to a $1.3 billion multi-tranche facility with over 20 lenders. (This is an 80-fold increase) I was also involved in a number of special projects and enjoyed a great deal of satisfaction from all of this work.

> Taught auditing at the college level for three years.

> Designed and taught a memory techniques course to people ranging from 3rd grade youngsters through those in their golden years.

> Designed and taught a time management course for some of our company employees.

> Worked almost continuously on various aspects of self-help and self-improvement. The material in this book is a very significant part of the results of this effort.

> Read over 1,600 books since 1972...mostly by listening at double speed on Audible.

> Had a thoroughly enjoyable evening sitting at an 8-person table with the former President of the Soviet Union, Mikhail Gorbachev. A picture of the two of us toasting each other is a prized item hanging on my study wall.

> I grew up without formal religious training of any sort, so I began in my early 20's to investigate this side of life. I subsequently studied several religions in depth – especially Catholicism, Christian Science, and Unity Church — and read The Bible twice, cover to cover.

> Studied *A Course in Miracles* for a number of years.

> Received neurolinguistics counseling and studied the ideas of NLP.

> Participated in est training and related programs for several years, including once clocking my best time for a mile run of slightly over six minutes during one of their multi-day programs.

> Helped a number of wonderful people through challenging times.

> Actively engaged with family members, including caring for dying parents and teaching my second mother-in-law to drive when she was 65.

> I played football throughout high school and was named co-captain of the team in my senior year.

> I enjoy watching football to this day, and I was well into my 40's before finally abandoning the fantasy that a New Orleans Saints home game would be stopped, and I would answer the call to come down and play linebacker for the team.

> Played a fair amount of baseball and softball.

> Took up skydiving briefly in my early 20's. I packed my own parachutes, learned parachute landing falls under the watchful eye of a former Viet Nam green beret, and climbed out of the plane onto a very tiny step holding only a wing strut to make my jumps. This was indescribably amazing!

> Enjoyed a number of zipline excursions.

> Rappelled down the face of a couple of cliffs (also cool!).

> Did a Tyrolean traverse across a canyon – this involved hanging horizontally from a harness below a steel cable face-up and pulling myself hand over hand across the abyss below.

› Paragliding.

› Bungee jumping.

› Hang gliding.

› Passenger in 2-person glider.

› Snow skiing, briefly.

› Snorkeling and scuba diving.

› Racquetball player for many years. I entered many tournaments, but I won only one tournament and that was against a great guy who just happened to be in a wheelchair. (This is a long story for another time.)

› Pretty much every beach ride or heart-stopping, pulse-racing adventure that was available to me. I've been spun, shot upward, dropped down, twirled and twisted in every possible way.

› A serial exerciser with a firm belief in physical activity.

› Coached 6-to-8-year-old youngsters in softball. I invented the practice of arranging the batting order alphabetically to reduce or eliminate the players clamoring to "let me bat first!"—but I am still waiting for this to catch on and work its way into the majors. I also developed the predictive algorithm which mandated that whenever these munchkins made it to third base, I would send them in to home plate. The infield throws at that age were pretty inaccurate, so it was a good bet that the kids would score.

› Bought a Porsche, my first sports car, at age 70 and then traded it after three years for another (a convertible) which I drove for two more years. During the Christmas season, my Porsche sported antlers and a red nose. It was a wonderful experience and I've never had more fun driving.

> Have owned over 50 cats in my life, with a high of five at one time. As a reminder as to why such a high number; I grew up across the street from a high school and the driving age at the time was 15, so our family, unfortunately, had a lot of turnover in terms of our feline pets.

> Have both held and played with actual tiger cubs on two occasions – once with only one, and the other time with five or six cubs playing and running around on top of a pool table.

> Went into a full-grown tiger's cage with a person who was armed only with a rubber Billy club. When given the invitation to follow him in, I did not stop to think it over; I just grabbed my camera and went in. It was very exciting!

> Been fortunate enough (with a lot of effort) to watch an NFL football game from the sidelines, directly behind the players. Also, I have been courtside for a number of NBA games. These experiences were wonderful, as you get a unique perspective of what is happening from down there.

> Drove 115 mph in a Ferrari on a racetrack.

> Drove 140 mph in a Lamborghini on a racetrack.

> Currently winning my lifetime battle with weight.

> I enjoy photography while spending time traveling and being in the mountains.

> I like reading or listening to books at double speed.

> Learning about and using technology such as smart phones, laptops, iPads, etc.

> Writing this book.

In short, life has been a very rich, exciting, and rewarding journey; and I certainly do not feel I have lived a sheltered or cloistered life in any way, shape, or form. I have simply made choices that made sense to me and which, I thought, furthered my goals and interests.

For me it was right thing to choose to focus on family, career, exercise, and general health, as well as mental health and spiritual matters. A different combination might be right for you; but my choices, while limiting my activities in some ways, let me focus on others to a greater degree.

I leave it to you, the reader, to decide if mine was a wasted or productive life. I fully understand that opinions may vary; but the only opinion that really counts to me is my own each night when my head hits the pillow. And I am happy to honestly say I feel that it has been a full and exciting life, one that allows me to feel both satisfied and proud.

APPENDIX B
A FOUR-PART MEDITATION

NOTE 1: THE PART NAMES and numbers are for your information only and need not be read as part of the meditation.

Note 2: Italicized words are my own personalization and can be replaced by you, the reader, with your own analogous information, descriptions, etc.

Note 3: You are free to add or subtract other portions to make this meditation as meaningful as possible to you.

Part 1 – Breathing and Relaxing

Alright, *Howard*, I want you to

Close your eyes

Take several deep breaths, cleansing breaths...

A warmth comes over you, relaxing you completely.

Pay close attention to your breathing:

When breathing in, think of taking in

Calm,

Peace, and

Relaxation

As you breathe out, think of ridding yourself of

Tension,

Worry, and

Anxiety

So that just the act of breathing helps you to relax more completely.

You feel totally relaxed

Loved, and giving love to others;

Accepted, and accepting others;

Forgiven, and forgiving others.

You feel grateful for all of your blessings.

You feel

No stress,

No fear,

No anxiety.

You are totally relaxed.

You know that you can relax anytime, any place, and under any circumstances – it's entirely within your control.

Part 2 – Special Place

Now when you are calm and at peace, begin to go to your special place ...your favorite spot; almost sacred, hallowed.

You follow a beautiful, cobblestone path lined on both sides with centuries-old, moss covered oaks which provide an arched canopy well overhead.

The air is cool, crisp, and dry. The sky is a beautiful blue, and the surroundings are so quiet that you can hear acorns drop from time to time.

the path leads to a lush forest with

giant redwoods and sequoias – huge and majestic:

the biggest is 276 feet tall,

27 feet in diameter at the base,

2300 years old!

with 4 huge branches off of the main trunk ... each the size of a large tree by itself.

there are 2 billion leaves,

and the trees are continually adding new growth to their circumference and height.

these trees leave you in a state of awe and wonder.

You look around at your surroundings:

the light is dim due to the trees blocking the sun.

you hear the gentle rustling of the forest—the wind, birds, and other animals;

and you hear a brook or stream in the distance with its nice, soft, peaceful sound.

there is a light "foresty" smell—- crisp and clean.

You stay as long as you like, drinking it all in;

And you realize that you can return here anytime .... No matter the physical location of your body, and no matter the conditions surrounding you.

Part 3 – Seeing Your Entity

Now, after enjoying this, you begin to look off into the distance ....

You see someone or something – it could be a real person, an animal, or someone who is not currently of this world.

You see your *tiger*;

You watch him approach;

You rub and scratch his face, then under his chin, and behind his ears; you pet his stomach and sides.

You nuzzle him like a dog or cat lover would do with a pet.

You smell him, take in his scent, breathe on him; and he does the same with you.

You hear him make contented noises, and you purr back.

You roll around with him, play and scratch and rub him.

And you receive the message he has come to give you:

Your world is accepting and welcoming ...

You need have no fear or anxiety ...

You can experience total peace and joy ...

You have good health ...

You give and receive love, acceptance, and forgiveness ...

You have gentle strength, and power ...

You have determination ...

> *And you have the ability to make choices that are, and will be, correct for you, and will support your goals and desires.*

You stay for as long as you like and eventually realize that it is time for your *tiger* to leave, but you know *he* is always there, waiting for you – you can be with *him* at any time, and in any place that you are.

Part 4 – Release

Now you hear the stream in the distance that you had heard earlier, and you go toward it ....

You see the stream flowing nicely, producing gentle sounds, flowing evenly and steadily over partially submerged rocks.

The water is very clear and clean.

You take off a burden you are dealing with.

In your case, it is the *excess weight you are carrying – you take off the weight jacket that holds this and covers the body you want to have.*

As you do this, however, you notice that *the jacket has several pockets and you decide to use* them to unburden yourself of potential negative emotions.

> You put all of your excessive anxiety into *one of the pockets.* You are strong and capable; trust yourself; celebrate yourself. Choose to let go of excessive anxiety. It serves no constructive purpose, and it is best gotten rid of.

> Next, you look for any and all anger and resentment you may still be carrying. You realize that most people are trying to do a good job and don't mean to cause resentment or anger. You also realize that anger often reveals something about you or is a reaction to a perceived inadequacy, weakness, embarrassment, frustration, disappointment, hurt, extreme worry or fright, or a skill you feel you are missing. It can also be the effect of having unresolved conflicting feelings or being disrespected, unappreciated, or unfairly treated. Finally, your anger could be from being put in unpleasant, unfair, or otherwise avoidable situations, having your goals blocked, or feeling powerless. You accept this and commit to working on these issues as needed. You place your anger and resentment *in a separate pocket* and choose to be free of them.

> Then you find all of your fear and lovingly put that *into another pocket,* knowing that the feeling of fear will always pass. You recognize that you are more than capable of handling whatever comes your way. It is ok. Allow yourself to let go of fear and relax.

> Following this, you find all of your guilt and shame and gently place it *into the next pocket*. Once you have done all you can to make things right, and learn to do things differently in the future, you can choose to let go of guilt and shame. Stop beating yourself up. Hold your head high and follow the advice you would give a friend: Let it go.

> Next you take all of your sorrow and sadness, and put it *into yet another pocket*. It really is alright to move on; it does not help to hang on to sadness or sorrow. The good things that happened, even though they may be gone now, will always remain; and you need never forget them. You have much joy ahead of you in the future. You have paid your dues; allow yourself to be happy now.

> Finally, you review your life to find your regrets, and you put them *into the last pocket*. It is best to feel free of them, and you choose to let them go as well. They add nothing to your life. What is done cannot be changed; and you have the correct focus on the future and the skills to handle similar matters differently now.

Remember that these negative emotions are only a state of mind. They do not exist outside of your head, and cannot be found out in the universe.

They are likely to leave you as quickly as they have come, and you have the power to rid yourself of them, or greatly lessen their effect on you.

From time to time almost everyone has these feelings and you are not alone.

For yourself and for the others involved, you do all that is possible to heal and mend these hurts and negative feelings – apologizing, changing, or atoning in any appropriate ways for your part in these situations.

You think of the *weight* and all of the negative feelings as though they were people, and you forgive them and thank them. They are just trying to:

Help you,

Protect you,

Improve you,

Defend you,

Remind you,

Teach you new lessons,

And help you cope with situations in the only way they know.

Remember that even the worst negative thoughts and uncomfortable feelings allow us to grow and learn in the future, and set us apart from all other animals.

You are your own "Greatest Miracle" and you can follow the core principles:

Count your blessings,

Proclaim your rarity,

Go the extra mile,

Use wisely your power of choice,

Do all things with love – for yourself, for others, and for god.

Now, you bend toward the stream and let go of *the jacket*, with these negative feelings and your *excess weight*.

You watch the *weight jacket*, as well as all the negative feelings, slip away – they partially dissolve, partially submerge, and partially just get further and farther away – mentally and physically.

This is a wonderful, freeing feeling!

You feel prepared to be the most fully functioning, capable person you are able to be—loving, kind, and helpful, to others and to yourself.

There is no ego involved, just a warm feeling of love and joy, and a very high level of gratitude.

You know you can stay as long as you like and come back anytime; but after fully enjoying this experience, you realize it is time to return.

You take a few more deep and relaxing breaths, and then, when you are ready, you open your eyes.

APPENDIX C
FURTHER THOUGHTS CONCERNING THERAPY

SELECTING A THERAPIST

There are a variety of educational backgrounds, specialties, and experience levels to consider, and it may pay to interview more than one therapist before making your decision. You want to be sure they have experience and qualifications in the areas you think you are interested in. But like just about everything else in life that involves people, there is a wide range of styles, competencies, and approaches among therapists. Remember that your initial decision in favor of a given person is not a life-long commitment; and changes can always be made. Trust your judgment and your intuition; pick someone you are very comfortable with and with whom you seem to have the best rapport. This can prove to be more important than the degrees they may have.

I have experienced a full range of results with psychiatrists, and my results have generally been extremely productive. My experiences with psychologists and social workers have been similarly productive.

It is best to be totally open, honest, and upfront with your therapist, and to communicate fully with them from the very beginning. I don't think you can go wrong with this approach, but you may find it to be challenging at times. That's okay and to be expected. Sometimes the benefits are not obvious during the process.

Even if you decide eventually to make a change in therapists and worry you may have wasted some time and money on the therapist who wasn't the right fit for you and your issues, know that the efforts you've made are worth it to achieve your ultimate goal. While doing this does not always feel like the most direct or efficient process, in all likelihood you will get to learn and see different things by working with different people, even if you end up covering some of the same life experiences. Besides, Larry the lab rat may never really understand the therapeutic process, nor is this required, so just keep working on finding someone you feel comfortable with and let them guide you. Keep in mind that it is pretty common to wander into all sorts of surprising topics during the course of your work together.

Also, you may like to prepare some questions to ask any potential therapist going into the initial interviews. Perhaps there is a question or two you might have that really constitutes a litmus test; their answers may be very meaningful for you.

One of my requirements, at least half seriously, is that I prefer to work with a person who likes and has pets, especially cats. This may not sound telling to some people, but for me it is a requirement. I probably would not work with a therapist who disliked cats. You may have your own benchmarks. And you might feel you could only work with, or work best with, someone who _________________ (you fill in the blank.).

One of the differences among therapists I have found meaningful is their level of input. Some prefer to draw you out with a traditional series of comments like "Tell me more about that ...." This seems like a Socratic, or Freudian approach whereby you do most of the talking and discover your own truths with their direction. I personally prefer a more interactive approach in which the therapist is more of an active participant in the discussion.

Put another way, I have jokingly offered a (neoprene) bat to at least one therapist and invited her to tap it lightly in her hand or whack me with it if I'm missing the point, not getting the lesson, gone too far astray, or not dealing with a topic appropriately. I value feedback and being challenged on any incorrect or counter-productive attitudes or thought processes I may have.

For example, one time I was describing what I had done and said in a particular situation, and my very wise therapist at the time told me that he could "...just see my wife loading her figurative gun as I spoke, getting ready to blast me." I've evaluated many situations since then with this in mind, and it has been a helpful tool for considering how some of my normal responses may seem to others.

While you may be more comfortable with a highly interactive, discussion-type regimen, bear in mind your therapist may know that their input beyond a certain point may not be the most productive approach. Remember also that you won't even know what is actually helping all of the time. We may think we do ... but that is not always the case.

My experience has been that therapists, for the most part, are angels on earth! They are caring and knowledgeable people who will do their best to be of help. I have worked with approximately 16 of these good souls over almost 70 years, and with the exception of one fellow who was relatively unhelpful (and who, I believe, made an unethical request), I absolutely know that I have learned and grown a great deal thanks to this work. I have worked with psychiatrists, psychologists, social workers, and marriage counselors (not simultaneously!), and I feel very blessed to have known and worked with almost all of them. They have been instrumental in many of the positive changes I have achieved. It is for this reason that I normally leave a really great cake in the lunchroom of my therapist's office for the holiday season with a note saying: "For the few who do so much for so many."

———⬤———

BEGINNING THERAPY

You need have no real concern about how to begin therapy and what to say or bring up during your first sessions, although I can easily understand that many people may. We all wish we did not have problems sufficient to cause us to seek help, but it's pretty much a given that we do at the point that you show up for the first time. My advice here is to do your best to stick to "I" statements and try not to blame others, even though I know we often fervently wish to blame others for our stress. Also skip the "why I do not need to be here," or the "how great things are" listing of how wonderful everything is, except this one tiny little area ... ! Just let your thoughts and feelings flow during your session.

Here are some sample questions to initially get you thinking and talking:

> What makes me sad?

> What hurts my feelings?

> Why do I feel guilty?

> What do I regret?

> What have I done that causes me to feel shame?

> What causes me to feel strong negative emotions?

> In what circumstances do I have trouble acting rationally?

> In what situations do I become anxious or fearful?

> What do I value?

> What's missing in my life?

> What do I crave more of?

> What makes me angry or resentful?

> What embarrasses me or makes me feel uncomfortable?

This list could be much longer, of course; but the questions make for a good starter kit. By the time you address these questions, any others they bring to mind, and/or others that are specific to you, you should be well along the way in your journey.

SORRY, BUT NO GUARANTEES!

With the potential and power of therapy as a strategy for combating excessive anxiety and/or other emotional issues, it would be nice if there was a guaranty of effectiveness and help for each person who suffers. Unfortunately, no such guarantee exists in the real world! There are too many variables for this to be realistic, such as the following:

> The patient's ability to follow the program,
> The willingness to face issues and work through them,

> The patient's willingness to change.
> The patient's ability to be open and objective.

Despite these realities, a goal of very significant improvement is very likely to be achieved. Successes are infinitely more common than failures. You have every reason to be positive and optimistic about making major progress with therapy. In fact, I have never heard, nor have I even read, of anyone who sought help this way who said therapy was not worth the time or effort. To me, this is very significant!

QUOTES ABOUT THERAPY

To demonstrate further support for therapy, I have included comments from two well-known people:

> In his memoir at age 67, Bruce Springsteen, discusses his family ties and his path to mental health:

"When I first started to get help for depression and anxiety, I was very uncomfortable. I was 32. I look back and think, 'What was all the fuss?' Now it's something I don't mind talking about. Therapy has been very helpful, along with psychopharmacological medicines that allowed me to be more effective in my family life and more present in my family life and more present in the world. It's been a huge part of my life experience."

AARP Bi-Monthly Magazine / Bruce Springsteen's memoir, *Born to Run*, was published in September by Simon & Schuster.

> Susan Williams, Robin Williams`s wife – Public statement after Robin's death:

> "Robin wanted us to laugh and be unafraid ... his greatest legacy besides his three children is the joy and happiness he offered to others, especially those fighting personal battles. He was brave as he battled with his own depression and anxiety, and the initial stages of Parkinson disease which he was not yet ready to share

publicly. It is our hope in the wake of Robin's passing that others will find the strength to seek the care and support they need to treat whatever battles they are facing so they will feel less afraid."

It is not an exaggeration to say that, in serious cases, therapy can save a person's life. This brings to mind a cartoon showing a doctor standing beside an overweight patient and asking him, "What fits best into your busy schedule— exercising an hour a day or being dead?" It can be like that with therapy too, except that therapy is generally only an hour a week.